MARRIED R E *for* A L

More Praise for *Married for Real*

"Jerome and I thoroughly enjoyed reading *Married for Real*. The more we read, the more we enjoyed it. Taj and Eddie allowed themselves to be transparent by openly revealing their troubled pasts and informing us on what it has taken for them to have a happy, healthy marriage. We appreciated having Taj and Eddie share their individual voices by writing their own points of view, which ultimately translated into one voice—the voice of mutual love, respect, spirituality, and togetherness. The questions throughout the book had us engaged in great conversation and allowed us to reconnect on issues that lay dormant after five years of marriage. We consider *Married for Real* a must-read for any individual or couple who wants a fresh relatable perspective on having a meaningful relationship with a strong foundation."
—Jerome and Trameka Bettis

"This is a great book. Even for my own happy marriage, I found some golden nuggets for us too. Thank you, Eddie and Taj! God bless you and thanks for setting the record straight about the importance and value of marriage."
—Diane Wells, mother of Reggie Wells of the Carolina Panthers

EDDIE & TAMARA GEORGE

MARRIED

R E *for* A L

BUILDING A LOVING, POWERFUL LIFE TOGETHER

with **Rob Simbeck**

Abingdon Press
Nashville

MARRIED
R E *for* A L

Library of Congress Cataloging-in-Publication Data

George, Eddie, 1973-
  Married for real : building a loving, powerful life together / Eddie and Tamara George with Rob Simbeck.
    p.   cm.
  Includes bibliographical references and index.
  ISBN 978-1-4267-2248-6 (hardback : alk. paper) 1. Spouses—Religious life. 2. Marriage—Religious aspects—Christianity. I. Johnson-George, Tamara A. II. Simbeck, Rob. III. Title.
  BV4596.M3G46 2012
  248.8′44—dc23

                                                                        2011035632

12 13 14 15 16 17 18 19 20 21—10 9 8 7 6 5 4 3 2 1

MANUFACTURED IN THE UNITED STATES OF AMERICA

CONTENTS

GEORGE FAMILY
MISSION STATEMENT

Our mission is to provide a well-balanced and happy environment in which our family can flourish and grow without limits with God as our foundation.

INTRODUCTION

In the beginning, there were Adam and Eve. You've heard that story all your life, right? Well, it's not exactly true. First there was Adam, all by his lonesome.

Now, Adam learned to survive without a companion. He didn't ask for much or complain that his emotional needs were unmet. Maybe he was so engulfed in his love for God that he never thought about a companion.

It was God who decided to do something about the situation. He said, "It is not good that the man should be alone" (Genesis 2:18). So, while Adam slept, God took a rib from his body and created little Miss Eve, and we all remember the rest of the story because, in so many words, that's when it all hit the fan.

Everything changed when the population of Eden doubled from one to two. It seems that whenever you put two people with their own emotional needs into any situation—even paradise—there's bound to be a difference of opinion at some point, and there's going to be a clash. In this case, Adam may still have been content, but Eve was looking for something more. So how did

Adam react? Well, the pressure of keeping Eve happy led him to break one of God's sacred rules, and the consequences forced them out of their beautiful home.

What if Adam and Eve had had some kind of mediator or a manual on living happily ever after, something more than just an order to stay away from that tree? Can you imagine what would have happened if Eve had put Adam's needs and concerns first or at least had considered them *before* she took that God-forsaken fruit? Things would probably be very different for you and me as far as relationships are concerned.

This book is meant to be that kind of relationship manual. It grows out of the realities of the life we have shared since, by the grace of God, we found each other. Now, right up front we need to tell you that it wasn't always peaches and cream. In fact, if it had been, this might be a very dull book—and it wouldn't be very helpful. It took us five years to begin to get it right, and even then we stumbled a few times. Fortunately, the divine intervention that brought us together seemed to keep us connected through it all. Over the course of those early years, our paths crossed three times— in delight as well as in fury. It's clear that some people just don't get it right on the first or second try. Our third meeting was the charm that began our life together. At that point, something just clicked, and we wanted "it" more than we wanted to be without "it."

All those starts and stops along the way, the delayed opportunities and missed connections we dealt with, taught us valuable lessons about life and love that we are here to pass along to you. This book attempts to bridge the gap between your wants and needs and to help you create a better atmosphere for developing a strong, stable, and meaningful relationship. It's designed to help people customize productive marriages that are just a little closer to "happily ever after" than they might be otherwise.

Are we relationship experts? No. Do we have degrees in psychology or counseling? No again. But we believe we have something worth saying. We each bring a lifetime of relationship experience to this book, and we've got thirteen years of togetherness that have taught us what it takes to make a relationship work. Could we have benefited from a book like this? Absolutely! That's one of the big reasons we wanted to do it. We know how important it is to hear from real people who've been through good and bad and come out the other end united—and smiling!

GETTING REAL

For whatever reason, most books like this don't get real. Anyone who knows us knows that we are *definitely* real. That's not something we have to work at. It's just who we are. And so we've done our best to bring that to the table. You'll get to see us, warts and all. We'll talk about real situations and real outcomes. This is life, not fairy tales. But we're hoping that you can learn from everything we've been through and that you can sort through the laughter and the tears and pick up some tips for building your own great relationship.

Back in 2007, we appeared in TV One's reality series *I Married a Baller*, which gave people nationwide a chance to see how we juggle family and our very different careers. We can't begin to count the e-mails we've gotten since then or the times people have stopped us in person to tell us what a perfect couple we are and how "together" we seem to have it. It cracks us up! They don't see the rough patches we go through or the times when we disagree on something major—or something minor!—or how long it can take us to come to an agreement.

It doesn't occur to them that we're just like everybody else. One of the things we like about doing this book is the chance to show people that perfect is unrealistic. Although we're not perfect, we do have a great relationship, and you can have one too, even if it doesn't seem that way at the moment. We're just two people with very hectic lives who are in love and want to make our love work, day by day. If we can find time to use these rules and keep it together, you can too. Yes, it'll take a little work, but a great relationship is worth any effort you put into it.

SIMPLE, DOABLE RULES

Most manuals overload you with pages and pages of rules and guidelines. To put this manual to work in your relationship, you will only have to master six very doable rules:

1. Find and Polish the True YOU—You'll work on yourself as a person, cleaning up your baggage and chipping away at the faults that get in the way of a good relationship.

2. Put in the TIME—You'll learn to take the time to create and develop a strong foundation for your relationship.

3. Live by FAITH—Your relationship with God is the backdrop to a good relationship with your partner. You'll learn the basics of accountability for the things you do because you're living not just for yourself but for a higher power.

4. Handle Your MONEY—Money is at the root of more arguments than almost anything, and this chapter will help you find ways to avoid unnecessary money woes.

5. Practice the Art of SEX—You'll learn that sex is an expression of a deeper and more inclusive intimacy. We'll talk about why it's important to take your time and seriously consider your commitment to each other before getting to this stage rather than jumping headfirst into an activity that's the equivalent of Eve's fruit. We might as well say it now: we had a sexual relationship before we were married. We were at a different place in our lives and our faith. As we continued to grow in our faith walk, we noticed that physical intimacy for us was so much better once we were married. But we promised to be real, and we will tell you the truth about our relationship all the way through.

6. Build the POWER of ONE—When two people use these rules to build a meaningful adult relationship, they come together and express themselves as a unit—a partnership that's better than the sum of their parts—even as they retain their unique identities.

We'll devote a chapter to each of these concepts, showing you, step-by-step, how to turn the baggage-carrying you who starts the journey into half of a powerful, loving couple. This book is also an opportunity for a self-check—a chance to look at yourself and delve into the fears or other negative emotions that may be holding you back from reaching your potential as an individual and as a relationship partner.

There will be growing pains. Everyone goes through them. But with these steps, you should be able to get through anything. Maybe Adam and Eve didn't learn some of these things in time, but through trial and error, tears and laughter, we have learned them. Now, we're hoping you can learn them too.

And make no mistake about it—we practice the things we're urging you to do. We're in our seventh year of marriage and our thirteenth year as a couple. We regularly assess where we've been, where we are, and where we're going. This time, we're just inviting you along! This book is our chance to reaffirm our values, to revisit where we've been and look to where we're going as a couple, and to determine how we can support each other in that.

We wrote this book together, as a couple. Wherever you see plain type, like this, that's the two of us talking. But we're still individuals, with our own stories and our own points of view. We each have important things to say, as a woman and a man, and as Taj and Eddie. We want to bring our individual perspectives to this book, so here's how we do it.

When I've got something I want you to know from my point of view, or when I've got a story to tell about the subject at hand, I'll use italic type, like this. —Taj

And when I've got something to bring to the table, I'll use bold type, like this. —Eddie

Are you ready to receive a relationship? Are you ready to grow it slowly and lovingly into what God wants you and your partner to have? Then let's walk together.

If there is one thing I want you to take away from this book, it is that growing up means learning the difference between what you want and what you need. So many people want fairy-tale love, and there's no such thing. We need to concentrate on what's real, for men and for women. —Eddie

If there's one thing I want you to take away from this book, it's that you're getting the real us here. When I first talked to Eddie about this, I said, "If we're going to do a book, we have to bare our souls and show people that we're not perfect and that we haven't always known what we were doing from the beginning." He said, "Yeah, of

course. We have to tell the truth." And I said, "Even if it makes you look bad?" He was like, "Yeah, even if it makes me look bad."

That's one of many reasons I love him. He's real. And he's willing to work on himself and on us, even if the process can be messy.

Then he laughed and said, "How do I look now?"

After all these years, I thought he looked pretty good. That's another reason I love him. —Taj

CHAPTER ONE

FIND AND POLISH
THE TRUE YOU

What I had to do for myself, and what I encourage other

people to do, was to figure out my faults and where they

came from. I had to try to improve on those qualities or at

the very least try to keep them from affecting our relation-

ship. That way, working on me becomes working on our

relationship!—Taj

We could have called this chapter "You and Your Baggage." All of us have it. We certainly do. A few people seem to travel light—women with maybe a handbag's worth, just enough to get through a night on the town, men with not much more than you could toss into the glove compartment. Others travel like they're moving across the country, with more cases, trunks, and bags than you could cram into a U-Haul, lugging all kinds of drama, fear, and regret into every new situation. Most of us, we think, are somewhere in the middle. We all wish we could travel lighter, and we're not willing to unpack everything, especially in front of that special someone we've just met and hope to start something brand new with.

We all have "histories." That's what makes us who we are, good, bad, or indifferent. And whether or not we want to acknowledge it, that history has shaped our ideals and our wants and needs. The reality—and remember, we're being real here—is that we'll never get rid of all our baggage permanently, but the two of us are living proof that it's possible to minimize it, to turn liabilities into assets and negatives into positives.

This chapter is about working on *you* because that's where all your relationships start. A healthy you is the basis for any healthy relationship. When you're in a good place, your mate is more likely to complement you than to clash with you. Now, in order to become the best possible you, you have to face the you that exists now—and that means learning to see both the good and the bad. In this chapter, we will teach you how to recognize and pump up your best qualities as well as acknowledge and improve upon your bad qualities so that you're able to accept the love that God has placed in your life.

I can honestly say that both Eddie and I travel with a lot less baggage than we used to. We both had some from our childhoods and the relationships we'd been in before, but I think most of his came at the end of his NFL career, at that point where he had to adjust to a brand-new life. I'm proud to say he's worked through that. I don't think he's carrying much more than you could fit in a fanny pack. As for me, a lot of stuff still pops up, and I can get very emotional on short notice. Sometimes Eddie talks me down out of the tree, and sometimes I can coach myself out of it. But where I used to have a mountain of luggage, therapy and the kind of work we're talking about in this book have helped me cut it down to just a backpack! —Taj

My idea of family was shattered at the age of five when my mom and dad divorced. I really didn't know why they were splitting up, but I thought it was because of me...because I didn't help my mom with the chores around the house. As sad as that is, that's what I thought. No child of five can really understand what splits up their parents' marriage or what adults are capable of thinking or doing. All I knew was that a spike had been driven through the family, and I still carried the thought that I had caused it. As the years went by, the relationship between my mom and my sister was affected also. They just didn't get along. My family was dismantled for reasons I didn't know at that time.

My mom was a flight attendant, and she was gone a lot. My sister and I lived with our grandmother most of the time while I was in grade school and high school, and we only saw our mom on the weekends.

My father was in and out of my life a lot during those years. He lived right around the corner from me, but he was emotionally unavailable. My father's distance had a big effect on me and eroded my confidence and self-esteem and chipped away at my very identity.

During those years, with no one I viewed as a real disciplinary figure, I became quite the little menace. I wasn't doing things like stealing or robbing people—it was more like skipping class or skipping school altogether, not studying or applying myself academically. I didn't care about school. I cared about football. That's where I poured all my dreams.

What kept me grounded through all of it were the people around me—my mom, my grandmother, and my uncles, Kevin and Derek. They were the ones who said that I could accomplish something, that I could be somebody. They were the ones who said, "Here are the possibilities."

My mom saw what was happening and decided after my sophomore year at Abington High School in Philadelphia to send me to Fork Union Military Academy in Virginia. She saw my potential, the part I was using and the part I was wasting, and she made a huge financial sacrifice to send me away to school.

It was there that I was given the opportunity to change my perception of what my life could be. My football coach was a huge anchor in my life at that time. He challenged me and pushed me hard. He told me I could be a Division 1 running back, maybe even a Heisman Trophy winner.

All of us have good and bad influences battling inside us, and despite the people who were pushing me to do well, it was very difficult for me. I put a lot

of defense mechanisms in place just to survive because there had always been other people and situations that were negative when it came to what I was doing or wanted to accomplish. Those defenses would stay with me well into my adulthood. —Eddie

I grew up in a violent household with a stint of molestation from a cousin. My stepfather, who came into my life when I was three years old, was a serious drug addict who was physically abusive to my family—mostly to my mother. To go into detail about the abuse that he put my family through would require a book in itself. We'll save my stepfather and cousin for a to-be-continued autobiography. My biological dad died when I was nine, my mom when I was fourteen. My three brothers and I were then split up. I had to live with a cousin who was not nurturing at all. In fact, I pretty much lived the Cinderella story—the first part, before the fairy godmother. I was miserable and resented my mother for leaving us by ourselves. Something she used to say to us when we worked her nerves would haunt me in my sleep. She'd say, "Y'all better appreciate me now because when I'm gone, no one is gonna treat you like your mother." She was so right! I wasn't allowed to do anything. And I mean nothing! I wasn't allowed outside, I couldn't use the phone, and I wasn't allowed to work on the

weekends, which was tough because all of the fast-food jobs required at least one day during the weekend.

Living in a one-bedroom, one-bathroom apartment in New York City with six people was a bit crowded. That I could deal with. What I didn't like was having to clean up after those who were home all day and unemployed, especially since Monday through Friday I was attending school, followed by work. I had to wash dishes every day, no matter what time I came home, and clean the bathroom, which was about the size of a large closet. It was just horrendous for me. I wanted my fairy godmother!

To go into detail about my cousin would require a full section in my autobiography, so we'll save some of that as well. I had my complaints, but my brothers had it far worse than I did. My brother Henry had just turned eighteen, so no one in my family felt there was a need to take him in. Almost a year later, he joined the Marines hoping to find stability. My brothers Robert (seventeen) and Wayne (sixteen) were not so lucky. My grandfather drove them to Bristol, Pennsylvania, to live with Robert's father, who had been absent for most of his life. He gave them both twenty dollars and left. And I felt that my cousin acted like she'd been forced to take me, I annoyed her, and as a result, I always felt out of place. The family that should have loved and taken care of my brothers and me didn't even want us there.

The experiences with my stepfather and molesting cousin definitely shaped the way I felt about men and relationships.

There wasn't a healthy model anywhere to change my per-ception from negative to positive. Growing up, I can't remember seeing a couple who made me say to myself, When I have a boyfriend, I want my relationship to be just like that. Every person I knew was having some kind of physical or emotional abuse or marital problem.

I felt like I couldn't open up to anybody, so I closed myself off. It became hard to manage my emotions around people. When I did find someone who seemed to recipro-cate my love—who ended up being a boyfriend—I became so attached and overbearing that I think I just pushed him away. I was eighteen or nineteen and ready to be in love for the rest of my life. I realized later how crazy I must have seemed. I just wanted an incredible marriage and a family that I could depend on, and I would think, I've found it, every time I found a boyfriend who treated me nicely (at first). I would believe that with him my life could finally have some kind of foundation. Of course, there aren't many boys that age ready for anything like that, so I found myself sabotaging my relationships almost from the start. —Taj

None of us gets through childhood and adolescence without some baggage, some bumps and bruises to our psyches. Life is a contact sport.

Preparing ourselves for a great relationship doesn't require that we eliminate every bit of baggage. It does mean dealing with it and learning to handle the situations and emotions that could turn into new baggage. And it was a learning process for us. As we have grown and matured, in our faith especially, we see that our premarital sex had a cost. Once sex enters the equation, there is no going back. It is a game changer, and it could easily have turned into new baggage.

So, where do we start?

It all begins with facing your history, and there's no better way to reveal the past to yourself than with paper and a pen or that trusty computer keyboard. There are a couple of advantages to putting it down in black and white. First, writing forces us to think, which is something a lot of us don't like to do with potentially unpleasant topics. And second, it puts good and bad in perspective. Our problems feel bigger and more complicated when they're running around inside our heads. Putting them on paper usually lets us see that they boil down to a few simple emotions, or a few simple tactics we use that aren't working anymore.

When you begin writing, you'll be tempted to spend too much time on what other people have done. What's important is not, *What did they do?*—although you need to acknowledge that—but *What did I do?* People are going to say and do things that hurt you. Sometimes they mean to; sometimes they don't. But finding the best *you* doesn't mean dwelling on others' mistakes or misdeeds.

It means facing yours so you can change your actions and attitudes.

It's hard to say whether I even knew what a good relationship was when I was a kid. At this point, I'd say it should be stable and enjoyable, for starters. The primary relationship I saw as a kid was the one between my parents, and it wasn't either of those things. There was always a lot of tension. None of us knew what was going to happen from day to day, or how our lives might change at any second.

The one intact relationship in my family belonged to my grandmother and grandfather. My grandmother was pretty much the rock of the family. She was the one who prayed a lot. She was the one we'd go to with problems. My grandfather was strong and stern, but he didn't say a lot.

I was a late starter when it came to relationships. In junior high and high school, I didn't have a social life of any kind. Just didn't have one. I was trying to find where I fit in, and I didn't. I wasn't a nerd, but I sure wasn't cool. I didn't have a girlfriend, and I didn't really reach my potential as a cool guy or whatever you want to call it until later on. In fact, I was Mr. Irrelevant, Mr. Cellophane. I left Abington High School for Fork Union Military

Academy and then went back to my old school to visit a year later, and people didn't know I had left! These were my friends, and they hadn't realized I was gone!

I didn't date in junior high, and I sure didn't see a lot of girls in an all-male military school. I had very little experience being around or talking with women. The only real exposure I had was what I saw on television or heard from my friends. Consequently, I was really shy with females. People thought I was arrogant or stuck up, but in fact, I was just nervous.

When I got to college, I had my first real girlfriend. I was eighteen or nineteen years old, and I really wanted a relationship. Most of my freshman year I was either at her apartment or driving her car around; I wasn't involved in campus life. It was cool up until spring quarter when I looked around and I saw a plethora of females on campus. Then I said, "Wow! I'm a freshman, and I have three more years of this! Why be with one girlfriend when there are all these girls walking around?" Let's just say I broke it off quickly, and I didn't settle back down until I married.

And I was still dealing with the self-esteem problems and the other things I'd confronted as a child. Everybody saw a tough, physical, hard-nosed football player, but on the inside, I was afraid of failure, of going back to where I was. I was scared to death. —Eddie

I realized I needed to work more on me after my ex-boyfriend broke up with me. It was a tough, bitter ending to the relationship, and I refused to let go. I thought, Maybe he's just not thinking correctly. Maybe if I could just give him a couple weeks off and then come back, he'll realize that we love each other and that we're supposed to be together. *I was holding on to my personal dream of a strong foundation with someone who didn't want the same.*

Even when he started seeing other girls, I kept thinking, This is just temporary. He just needs to get this out of his system, and then we're going to be together forever. Once he realizes that they don't love him like I love him, of course he's going to come back to me.

I was on tour with Sisters with Voices, and I had to be in D.C. on this particular night. I hadn't talked to him in maybe two or three weeks, which was like an eternity, because normally I would call like four or five times a day. I decided to call him. He was excited to hear from me, and I was excited that he was excited. I was thinking, It's working! He's gonna love me! *He told me that he had a game that night and that as soon as he heard my voice he knew he was going to have a great game because I was his good luck charm.*

So I went off and did my show and came directly back to my hotel room. I turned on the TV because I wanted to see if he had a good game, and he scored thirty-four points! I was like, This is it! I am the good luck charm, and we

13

are going to be together forever. It's gonna work now! Thank you, God!

I picked up the phone and called him, so excited to talk to him and for him to tell me that this is going to work now. But his new girlfriend answered the phone. What was left of my heart just exploded into one hundred million little pieces. So I kind of pulled myself together because I didn't want to sound like I was going to cry—I knew that would push him away—so I said in my best voice, "I'm so happy for you. Congratulations." And I got off the phone as quickly as possible. I couldn't hold in my pain any longer.

And when I did let that pain go, I literally cried for three days straight. I mean nonstop. I would eat and cry, I would call people and cry, I would get in the car and cry, I would lie down and cry, I would exercise and cry, and then I would cry some more. And I realized it was because I had to cry him out of my system. It was a detachment because I knew I just couldn't put myself through that anymore. More important, I realized at that point that it wasn't him doing it. It was me doing it. I kept allowing him to drag me through the mud. I kept going back for more. I kept believing that something was there that wasn't there. Realizing that and facing it were the hardest things for me to do, but that harsh realization set me free.

The next day, the third day, I woke up, and I stopped crying. It was almost like I just dried up, like I didn't have another tear left to cry. And I realized that I had to call that day and sever all ties with this person who didn't want anything to do with me anyway. It's almost as if he was doing me a favor by putting up with me. That's when I made that call and officially broke up with him. I said, "I know you can't change, but I have to change for my sake. It's not healthy for me." I told him that we shouldn't talk anymore, that this was it. I never talked to him again.

At that point I began to heal. I started praying; I started meditating; I started thinking about the things I had done. I knew that anything that had gone wrong went wrong because I allowed it to, and it continued to go wrong because I continued to allow it. At any point during that relationship, I could have said, "I'm not taking this anymore. I'm leaving." But I hadn't been able to because I kept wanting, kept reaching for, the stability and the foundation that I had never had before. I thought I had both with him, but I finally realized that stability and a foundation couldn't possibly feel like that. Having them shouldn't hurt that way.

As I worked on me, I realized that my mistakes hadn't begun in the last months of the relationship or even halfway into it. They had begun at the beginning. I realized I couldn't be so overly in love the moment somebody said hi to me. I couldn't expect someone else to be my rock. I couldn't expect someone else to take me to that happy place I'd been trying to get to. No one else could fill that void in me. I had to do it myself. Then and only then would I be ready for a real relationship.

My journal was such an important part of my growth. It really helped feed the breakthroughs I had. My sensitivity and emotions were big problems for me in my twenties. I wrote day after day in my journal, and when I read what I had written, it was like it was asking me, Why are you being so sensitive? Why are you doing this? I literally wrote out everything I was going through every day, every emotion I felt, every bit of anger, every bit of happiness, everything. At some point, I realized I could be better, and then there came the day when I realized, I'm not as bad as I was before! It definitely didn't happen overnight—it took months—but I realized I was stronger mentally. I was able to walk outside and not care that I didn't have anybody. I was able to go to the Village and walk down the street with my dogs, and I didn't have to feel perfect. I didn't feel like I had to be "put on" twenty-four hours a day because it was not about what people thought about me anymore. It was about what I thought about me. I was beginning to feel better about myself.

That breakup forced me to work on me, and it happened just in time—in what I'm convinced was God's time. All the experiences I'd gone through became the lessons I learned as I worked on myself, and they became the basis for the me I carried into my relationship with Eddie. Those hard-won lessons allowed my relationship with Eddie to work, to grow into what it has become. If I was still the same weak, emotionally damaged person I was before that breakup, we never would have made it. —Taj

Where does baggage show up in a relationship? Lots of places. When it comes to you as a couple, it can take the form of an unexplained silence or a sudden outburst. It can be triggered by a topic of conversation or an activity that brings up old memories.

But just as often it comes up in dealing with others—with his buddies or her girlfriends. And there's probably no place where it can come up more powerfully—or do more damage—than with family. We've dealt with that, just like most everybody has. And what we've learned is that it's about boundaries. Family was there first, and there's a place for that love, for that relationship. It's not about choosing one over the other. But the Bible says that we are to leave father and mother and be joined together and become one flesh (Genesis 2:24). You leave home and come together, and nobody should be able to step inside that circle with you. That's where the boundary comes in. You are fully justified in asking outside family to step out of the circle that is yours alone.

Eddie is an entirely nonchalant, nonconfrontational person—it drove me crazy! And I had to make him see that.

One of the best examples I have involved his mother. Eddie and his mother always had a very close relationship, and I don't think she ever liked any of his girlfriends. When I came into Eddie's life, he had not had a girlfriend for longer than a year—no one ever lasted that long. So I don't think his mother ever took me seriously when I came into the picture, and I definitely don't think she expected me to last as long as I did. With everything that was going on with him, she didn't expect me to integrate into his life as well as I did and I think that made her uncomfortable. And rather than express that, sometimes she would just lash out. Eddie, being that this was his mom, didn't know how to manage the conflict, and like I said, he was very nonchalant about everything. His suggestion would just be to ignore it. Just ignore it! And I'm thinking, "How much can I ignore?" I tried to explain to him, "It's easy for you to just walk away and pay it no mind, but it's affecting me! How do I handle it? I can't because this is your mom. I'm expecting you to take that initiative."

It came to the point where I almost had to ignore her altogether. I would just not even be in the same room with her because it was that uncomfortable. And it was the baggage of his mom's emotional attachment that we really had to work on for years.

One Sunday we were at a Tennessee Titans game. The Titans used wristbands for family members to get back to the players after the game. Eddie's mom approached me and wanted the wristbands, but I hadn't made sure that everyone in the family had made it to the family section at that point. I was actually looking for Eddie's dad to make sure he was able to get back to see Eddie before I gave her the rest of the wristbands. Well, she just didn't want to hear it. She ordered me to give her those wristbands, and it exploded into a huge argument. *As we were going downstairs, I tried to walk away from her because she was really berating me. Finally she pulled me to the side and told me that I didn't know the difference between Ls—lust and love—and that her son would never marry a girl like me. I mean she just put me down.* It made me think, Well, she would know her son. Am I wasting my time here? *With her words she was able to reach my core where I stored what was left of my emotional need for stability. It made me sad because I felt like I had wasted four years, and maybe she was right. I started thinking about everything! Nothing had progressed. We were still in the boyfriend-girlfriend mode and he was still enjoying life and I was still living on the side, being patient and doing whatever I was doing to pass the time away. To make matters worse, his entire family was upset with me because of the way his mother told the story. I felt like an outsider again.* —Taj

When it came down to my mom and my girlfriends, it was always going to be a problem, no matter who came into the picture. Anybody I took seriously, Mom had an issue with. She would complain about her. So when it happened with Taj, I talked to both of them. I'd tell Taj, "Don't take that. Listen, you're a grown woman." I really didn't want to have to deal with it. I'd say, "Just let it roll off your back." And then I had a talk with my mother. I said, "Mom, this is my girlfriend. You need to get used to that fact." There was a situation after a game. They were arguing in the hallway about something stupid. I said, "This is my workplace. This is what I do. You don't have to like each other. You don't have to respect each other. But you have to respect where I work and what I do. Do not bring this to the stadium. Mom, this is the woman I'm going to marry. You don't have to like her, but you're going to respect my decision. If you don't want to be around her, then you need to stay away." —Eddie

Normally we all went to Eddie's restaurant after a game. We'd sit around and eat and hang out. But after what had happened, I thought, It's probably time for me to go now. This is not where I need to be. I just left and went back to his house. But then, after about two hours, he called me and said, "I hope you're OK. I know that my mom must have really done something for you to go off because you don't usually behave that way." I told him, "I just reached a point where I couldn't allow her to embarrass and berate me. I am thirty-one, not a child!" It was refreshing to know that he knew that I wouldn't be outright rude to his mom. I just felt that I could never win against her, and it wasn't a fun situation to be in.

From that point I made the decision to take care of me and get myself together to move on—I was seriously thinking of ending the relationship—because I didn't see any space for me between his mom and him and his family. They were there from the beginning and I was the new person, and the new person is always the first to go. I thought that person would more than likely be me. So, I decided to be proactive about it. I was going to go before they could push me out, and that would be that.

But somehow I guess maybe he realized that though I was not more important than his family, I was as important as his family, and that I was in fact now a part of his family. I'm assuming that maybe that was the day when he turned for the better also. As I was thinking, I need to go, he was following me, and I didn't even know it! —Taj

OUR ENGAGEMENT STORY

That was when we got engaged, and there's no better way for me to talk about overcoming the baggage that family can be than to tell that story. And it's a wonderful story. Guys, if you want to make a lasting—and I mean lifelong—impression on that woman in your life, take some notes on the way Eddie George handled his proposal. Someone may have done it better, but I'm not sure I've heard about it.

He set it up perfectly, unbeknownst to me. He took me

back home to Brooklyn to re-create our first date. After lunch, he wanted to go for a walk over the Brooklyn Bridge. (I would always tell him how I loved walking over the bridge.) About halfway over, I saw these three guys way off in the distance with this cute little puppy. I'm an animal lover, and I said, "Oh! Look at that puppy! We have to go pet him!"

"What puppy?" he said.

"It's way up there!" I told him. "Let's go." I stopped the guys and asked if I could hold the puppy. One of them said, "You sing, don't you?" I said yes, and he said, "Can we sing for you?"

"Sure!" I told them. They started, and I thought, These guys are good. And they're singing all my favorite songs! The next thing I knew, they all took off their jackets, and each one of them had a word airbrushed on his T-shirt. They read, "Will" "You" "Marry," when I turned around in shock, Eddie was on one knee, wearing a shirt that read, "Me," and he was holding the most beautiful ring I had ever seen.

I said, "This is the best engagement ever," and I started to hand the dog back. They said, "No. It's your puppy!"

He had planned out the whole thing, and I never caught on! The bridge, the singers, the puppy, the T-shirts. Amazing! To top off the day, he took me to dinner to celebrate. To my surprise, all of my closest friends and family were there—a lot of whom I hadn't seen in years. I still don't know how all of them kept it a secret—it may be the only one they've ever kept!

I was overwhelmed, and Eddie completely won me over at that point. He had done it all himself without any suggestion or direction or anything else. We were in tune with each other. I thought, This is no longer a boy! This is the man I want.

The important points were, first, he knew me. He knew the things that meant something to me. He knew how important New York and the puppy and those songs and romance were. Second, he made it about me. He wanted to be sure that I was comfortable and happy and surprised and that I felt loved and special—which I did! And finally, he knew this moment would be better if he included only my friends and family. He knew his family would be included in the wedding—they even helped me plan parts of it—but for this moment, it was all about me and it would be best if we did this without them.

That day, I realized that it was definitely going to be about us for the rest of our lives because we had a circle that nobody could break apart. On that day, he chose me over his family in a good, healthy way, and I loved him ten times more for that. He didn't push them away; rather, he put me at the center of his attention. He let me know I was the object of his desire. And he won me over for good. —Taj

WORKING ON YOU: TOOLS AND EXERCISES

Self-improvement is not a new concept. What is new is the ability to do it right! Here are some questions that will help you look at yourself and give you a way to conduct an inventory of what's good and bad about how you deal with relationships.

For the best results, get out that paper and pen or sit down in front of the computer screen. Ask yourself the questions here. If they touch a nerve, good or bad, write out your thoughts. Save what you write, because you'll want to refer to it later.

You're not going to nitpick, because you don't need to go over every little thing. You're looking for those things that really bother or resonate with you, that get in the way of your serenity, your self-esteem, and your relationships.

CHILDHOOD EXAMPLES

❦ Did I see positive relationships growing up?

❦ Did I see negative relationships?

❦ What were the big differences? What did people bring into good relationships that they didn't bring into the bad ones?

HOW THEY AFFECTED ME

❦ Is my view of relationships healthy? Do I understand that they involve two imperfect people who have to work at them?

❦ Am I willing to accept abuse or negativity in a relationship?

❦ Do I guard my emotions because relationships scare me?

❦ Do I expect relationships to fix me?

THE PERSON I'VE BECOME

❦ What are my strong points as a potential partner, the positive attributes I can bring to a relationship?

❧ What are my weak points?

❧ Is my life full of drama? Anger? Depression?

❧ Am I generally optimistic or pessimistic?

❧ Are there holes in my life that I think a relationship will fill?

❧ Do I have my own dreams and aspirations?

❧ Do I have the discipline and patience to work toward those dreams and aspirations?

MY RELATIONSHIPS

🦋 How have my relationships gone?

🦋 What has gone well?

🦋 What has gone badly?

You might also write down the things that make you angry and the things that you fear. Be specific! You're trying to get at the root of these things. There are reasons for fear and anger, and you can't be free of them if you don't face them. If you can't deal with anger when it comes to friends or family, it's not going to be magically easier when you fall in love—or take a hostage, as some people call the way that many of us handle our relationships. Honesty is the key to a better life.

If you get angry every time that certain person in your life walks through the door, stop and figure out why. Maybe it's obvious—he or she did or said something you find completely unacceptable. So ask yourself, *Do I still want to be in this relationship?*

Sometimes it's best to keep a distance, even with family members. Maybe you've bickered at each other so long, the real causes are lost, or it's a personality clash. In that case, just look at your side of the situation and fix what you can. Sometimes you'll find that just changing your attitude, apologizing if you need to, can go a long way toward making things better.

If you're not already journaling, these questions might form the start of a journal, which can be a very valuable tool in keeping track of who you've been, who you are, and who you're becoming. It's a great way to get perspective and maintain your sanity. And since these are the same tools you'll use in a relationship, you'll have a big head start if you can use them on yourself.

By the way, if you're saying, "I don't have time to journal," it might mean your priorities are out of whack, because all of us need a little time just for ourselves, to think, to meditate, to get centered. If you think you don't have time to write, that may be the best indication that you need to!

I've used writing not only as a tool to help me express some of the challenges I was having in forming a functional healthy relationship with my older son but also as an opportunity to look at those chal-

lenges from a totally different perspective and address the issues. I had Jaire when I was twenty-three and can now (at thirty-eight) recognize unhealthy behaviors that stemmed from insecurities that came out of my childhood. I wouldn't say it hurt our relationship, but it did create some tension. He lives with his mom, and not being with him on a day-to-day basis has been a challenge. Wanting that full-time experience with my son, and not having that, fed into some of my insecurities. There were times when I was being too much of a competitor, thinking I had to beat him in everything, to teach him how to be a winner. That philosophy was potentially damaging. As I wrote and looked at it truthfully, I realized I had to change my way of thinking and my approach. I had to let it go. I have a newfound respect for fatherhood, and I've looked for better ways to approach it. I had to look at my experiences with my father and grow from them. I wanted to make my father proud, regardless of his own battles and difficulties. I still loved, honored, and respected him. The power of the father figure is so potent. I'm more conscious now of healthier ways to interact with my family. As long as my sons are being guided correctly, I have to make the best use of the time I have with them. It comes down to spending quality time and giving them my best in that moment, whether it's by example or by word. That's what they look up to. I've got to

remember how important a father's role is in a son's life and bring my best to that relationship. —Eddie

You never know when or how your baggage will affect you. Not long ago I was watching The View, and they were talking about a boy who was attacked by bullies. It took me back to a day when my youngest brother and I were walking home, and these bullies bumped me as they went by. Then we saw them beating the fire out of this other young boy. I yelled, "Get off him!" and my brother said, "Shut up! Don't say anything!" The boy finally got away and ran across the street, with cars swerving and screeching, and then into a bodega. He called the police and the guys were arrested. All these years later I still think about how it could have been me and my brother getting beaten up. I think it still resonates with me because we didn't help the poor thing. We were afraid of being hurt. Baggage is funny that way. It can pop up out of nowhere when you least expect it.

So what do I do with something like that? Well, I've thought about the things I've been through that left me feeling helpless or angry, and I've thought about the ways I've learned to avoid those situations or if I can't avoid them, to be tough when I need to be. I realize that a lot of what happened to me in the past was because I was a weak, scared *little girl. Now I'm a very strong, adult woman. I'm very protective of my family, and I'm also protective of myself. I don't allow people to take advantage of me the way I used to. There are times when it may come across to some people as cocky or mean, but if that's the way I have to protect myself, so be it.* —Taj

Once you've answered all of these questions, look through what you've written and search for themes. Are you easily angered? Do you get too serious too quickly? Or on the other hand, do you never seem to get very serious because you're afraid of commitment?

Don't forget your strong points. Are you generally easy to get along with? Are you a good listener? Are you realistic when it comes to people?

Once you get into the habit of writing, you'll begin to see patterns emerging. You'll say, "I eat when I get worried," or "My mother drives me crazy. We can't seem to spend ten minutes together without bickering." You'll recognize the patterns and what's behind them if you're honest. Maybe you use eating as a way to distract yourself from the hard but necessary work of dealing with a stressful situation. Maybe you resent your mother's tendency to view you as a child.

Now it's time to think about what to do with all the information you've gathered. First, you may want someone to talk to. Maybe you've already got that trusted best friend or family member. With what you've learned by writing, you can ask that person to sit down and help you sort through your strengths and weaknesses, to see how you can build on the strengths and work on the weaknesses.

Maybe you've already been in counseling. Maybe you have someone in the clergy you talk to now and then. With the answers you get to these questions, you'll be better prepared to make good use of your time in these sessions or conversations. Working with professionals is great for many people, but the process of self-discovery might make a visit to a professional unnecessary. Before you go to a professional and say, "Fix me. I just feel crazy!" remember that a lot of people go to doctors of all kinds and expect to be fixed. And while professionals can be helpful, sometimes they just listen to you talk while you figure it out yourself. You can do that at home and save the co-pay!

Remember, you can't fix someone else's problem. It's enough of a job to fix your own. There are so many people who think they can fix their boyfriend's or girlfriend's drinking or drug or sex addiction problem. *If only I show him I love him. If only I can make her feel secure.* You can't do that. You don't have the power to fix someone else. Your power is over *you.* You do have the power to decide whether you can deal with that other person as he or she is or walk away.

And be sure to treat your search with a light touch now and then. Try to learn to laugh at yourself. We're all basically in the same boat—sometimes our weaknesses crowd out our strengths. If we keep a sense of humor, we're more likely to stay calm and sane enough to work effectively on ourselves. So cultivate your ability to laugh!

Then, of course, there is prayer. Just as we need someone on earth to talk to, most of us find we can't move ahead without a good, solid spiritual connection. Dust off your Bible. Or if you're a regular at prayer and meditation, take the results of your answers to these questions into your time with God. Ask for help with specific instances and weaknesses. As two people who know the power of prayer and meditation, we can tell you that you can use them to tap into God's strength and accomplish things you never thought you could.

I started reading the Bible in earnest at a point in my life when I needed it. I still read it daily. I became a fan of Psalm 119:97-99 (KJV), which says, "O how I love thy law! . . . Thy commandments hast made me wiser than mine enemies. . . . I have more understanding than all my teachers." Psalm 119:165 (KJV) says, "Great peace have they which love thy law." I love Ephesians 2:10 (CEB):

"We are God's accomplishment, created in Christ Jesus to do good things," and 2 Timothy 3:16-17 (CEB): "Every scripture is inspired by God and is useful for teaching, for showing mistakes, for correcting, and for training character, so that the person who belongs to God can be equipped to do everything that is good." —Taj

We also know the benefits of exercise and general fitness—you can't feel your best when you're out of shape. Your physical well-being affects your emotional well-being.

We'll deal more with these issues in later chapters. For now, if you've answered these questions honestly and taken a good, hard look at yourself, you've taken a big step forward. You've begun to deal with your baggage. Congratulations! And here it's good to remember that if you deal with it effectively, your baggage can be transformed and can become the basis for a new and better you.

CHAPTER TWO

PUT IN THE TIME

In this chapter, we'll deal with one of the most precious resources we have—time. More relationships fail because of time than anything else—because people fail to put in enough of it before committing themselves. It's almost impossible to know everything about a person in a few weeks or months, and yet every day people commit themselves to exclusive relationships after just a few dates. They move in together after a few months. And then they and their friends watch as the cracks develop and the walls of the relationship begin to crumble.

It doesn't have to be that way! We all know that relationships can last a lifetime. In fact, long-lasting relationships used to be pretty common. You can still find them, and there's something you can learn from them. The relationships that last have been developed to last. The couples took the time to get it right. They took the time to get to know each other.

That's exactly what we did, although as you'll see, our individual circumstances played a big role in that. We'll talk about what we learned as we eased into our relationship, about conversation, about trust, and about the art of resolving conflict.

It's *always* important to put good, constructive, quality time into a relationship, no matter how long you've been together. In this chapter, though, we will deal especially with the first days and weeks, months and years of a relationship.

One of the biggest relationship killers we've ever seen—and we know you see it as much as we do—is impatience. We've got plenty of examples just from the people we know.

Two people met in August and hit it off wonderfully. In just a few weeks, they were together all the time, with him spending the night at her house quite frequently. She had a daughter who lived with her, and our friend decided that she and her boyfriend were setting a bad example. By October, she had given him an ultimatum—"Marry me or else"—and so they got married. It wasn't long before the relationship hit a rocky patch. To those of us watching, it was obvious what had happened. They had never put in the time. They went from being acquaintances to being lovers too quickly. They never even got the chance to have their first good fight before they were married!

Another couple met and also jumped right in without taking the time to know each other. They had no real basis for communication and no way to find a balance when it came to their schedules or their needs. The second time he showed up late, she just exploded, and the relationship disintegrated before their eyes. They met just before Christmas and broke up by Valentine's Day. They never talked again.

MIXED MESSAGES

The truth is that the friend in the second example never knew what happened. She couldn't figure out why she and her boyfriend had gone so quickly from such incredible infatuation to a breakup. In the first example, the woman hadn't been in a relationship in a while, and she was really eager for one. The gentleman she met fit the description of what she was looking for and she jumped in—completely. He saw somebody who was sweet and nice and willing to do whatever he wanted, so it was perfect for him too. But then, as she let him know she wanted to move forward after just a few weeks, he started feeling smothered. He felt that he was being forced to do something he didn't want to do. So there were two people in the same relationship but on two completely different wavelengths. Plus, she wasn't sending the message she intended to send. She was thinking, *I've always wanted to be with somebody like you, but I don't want my child to get the wrong impression.* What she said was, "We need to get married right now!"

She could have said, "I've always wanted a relationship like this, but we might have moved too fast, particularly when we consider my daughter. Maybe you should move out so she doesn't see you here all the time. Let's be engaged for a while. Let's work to get to know each other better and then come together fully." That would have made perfect sense because neither of them was completely together at the time, but she didn't care about that. She had a picture of happiness in her head, and she thought making this relationship permanent was going to give it to her. The hard work that goes into *developing* a relationship wasn't part of the picture. She had a void in her life, and she thought she'd found something that would fill it. He was thinking, *She's forcing me to marry her now because she knows I don't want to stop seeing her. It's comfortable here with her, so I guess I'll go for it, even though I feel trapped.*

Both of them were looking right past the ingredients it takes to develop a good, solid relationship—time and work. They hadn't had time to get to know each other. They hadn't talked through what each was looking for and how they were going to make it work as a couple. His resentment and her frustration made for a perfect storm. When that happens, a couple can go to the heart of the problem and try to fix it by slowing down and getting to know each other, or they can break up, as so many do. That option is sad for both of them, and it's worse still for the children so often caught up in that cycle as innocent bystanders.

Both examples illustrate the central point of this chapter—there is no reason to rush into a relationship! Even if two people figure out pretty quickly that they'd like to move toward marriage, they need to realize how much there is to learn about each other and about the way their lives and personalities will interact. We see a lot of men and women in their midthirties who miss that point. They are still looking for perfection, for a fairy-tale relationship. Well, *every* relationship is made up of two real people, no matter how together or how perfect either one seems in that pure infatuation stage.

Getting to know someone—which is what you want to do before you commit to forever—takes time. Learning *anything* takes time, and a human being is about the most complex subject you can tackle. You need to see someone in a lot of situations. How is your partner in social settings? How does he react to disappointment? How does she handle success? How does he treat his family? How does she treat your friends? How is he with money? What are her dreams? and a hundred other questions. Yes, you can spend a lifetime learning all there is to know about someone, but you should have a pretty good start before you say, "I do."

We're talking about getting to know the person in every way—not just physically. We'll spend a whole chapter on sex, but the point now is that sex is not a highway to the kind of knowledge you need about your partner—and it can actually be a roadblock. You can spend hour after hour in bed and not know any more about your partner than you did beforehand.

TOGETHER TIME, ALONE TIME

The starting point for the kind of learning you need to do is conversation—lots of it, about all kinds of things. The two of us love talking, especially to each other. From our families to our faith, from the neighborhood to the world, the subjects are end-less, although like many people, we're very likely these days to talk about the kids and the dogs, who are always providing us with interesting—and funny!—material.

Then there's just watching your partner live life. You want to interact with each other, with friends and relatives, with the world. You want to socialize, have fun, learn, pray, do all the things that people who are in a relationship have to learn to do together. There'll be phone conversations, nights on the town, lunch dates, hanging out with friends. And there'll be special things that help you bond. One of ours, as silly as this might sound, is making up dance routines to our favorite songs. We have face-offs with other couples, like our friends Flex and Shanice Knox, doing kick-ball-change moves. It's exercise, fun, bonding, and competition all at the same time.

It's also important to remember that you need time apart. Spending twenty-four hours a day with someone too soon in a relationship is just asking for trouble and disappointment. It's easy to feel closed in and closed off. When there's nothing around you but this person, it's not hard to get bored or become irritated. Spending time apart helps keep your time together fresh. That's not the message society is sending, obviously, because so many people start clinging to each other so quickly these days, but it works. Couples who are up under each other can miss the mark because they don't give each other enough time to mature.

The time it takes to learn about each other will be different for each couple, but the point is that it doesn't happen overnight. A relationship isn't just highlights—romantic dinners, moonlit walks, gifts, and sex. It's two people living through life's everyday moments, good and bad. Getting there takes time.

I can't say that Eddie and I did it right on purpose in the early years. What happened was that we lived in different cities, and that kept us apart long enough for our minds and hearts to get together before our bodies could distract us too badly. That's not to say we weren't attracted to each other, but being apart, there was nothing for us to do but get to know each other mentally and emotionally, not just physically.

I was in school. Eddie was playing in the NFL. We made it a priority to see each other once a month or so, but most of our relationship at the time was conducted on the telephone. We had to learn to listen. We had to learn to deal with issues that came up. We had to love, fight, work things out, smooch—everything—over the phone. That allowed us a closeness few people can gain that quickly because we didn't have the bells and whistles of physical closeness to distract us. We talked and talked and talked, and that process took us to a whole new level of trust.

It also kept me from repeating mistakes I had made before. I was very broken, and I think it was good that we conducted our relationship long distance for the first four years because it didn't allow me to attach my life to his. I had to do my own thing because we were so far apart. Before, I would always kind of rush into relationships, hoping to establish something wonderful. That would lead me to sabotage them. Eddie was kind of the opposite. He wasn't in a hurry to go anywhere. He was enjoying his freedom and all the perks that went with being a superstar running back in the NFL. With us being apart, I had the time and space to put all of those things into perspective and realize I didn't have to be the way I had in the past. I didn't have to love him to death. I could just love him for the moment. Being away from him, I was able to correct some of the mistakes I'd been making.

I believe we were supposed to be in a long-distance relationship in the beginning. I don't think we would have worked as a couple if we'd been in the same city from day one. There would have been too many issues, too many things I would not have been able to avoid emotionally, and I think that would have sabotaged us. But because we were apart, I had the chance to deal with myself, with the things I'd been through, as I learned to deal with him. It also gave him time to do what he was doing as he learned to deal with me. All of that allowed us to grow as a couple. —Taj

Living in different cities was a good thing for us because it took sex out of the equation. Often people fall in love because they're enamored with the physical aspects. They feel as though that's going to last a lifetime, but then the reality slaps you and the novelty of the sex slowly goes away. You start seeing and dealing with the human being; moods and behaviors come into play. Being sexually compatible is just a fingernail on the hand of marriage. You ask yourself, *What else is there? Where is this going?* You have to have something more substantial to bring to the relationship than great sex. It begins with verbal communication, great meaningful in-depth conversations that keep you up all night. Then at some point, you have to assess whether your partner is an asset or a liability. What are they bringing to your life—professionally, spiritually, and emotionally—that adds value? How do they respond in times of adversity? Do they support your dreams and goals? Or are they a liability and an energy drainer, not bringing anything that will enhance your life, individually or together? Taj and I had eight- to twelve-hour conversations about anything from daily activities to life aspirations. We took the time to get to know and understand each other. Taj and I realized we were both assets to each other. We shared the same mind-set. Yes, we were physically attracted to each other, but it was more of a spiritual

connection. We realized the potential. I saw the potential in her as a strong woman, that she could be a great mother. I always looked for strong motherly instincts in a woman. I looked for a strong and solid foundation, and she has that. —Eddie

THE ART OF CONVERSATION

Our society seems to have forgotten how to communicate face-to-face. Thirteen years ago we were building our relationship three thousand miles apart from each other, so the phone was our lifeline. We would literally fall asleep on the phone sometimes. Whenever we were together, our talks would continue from wherever we had left off. But in general, it seems there is less time for quality conversations now. There was a time when families, friends, and courting couples spent evenings talking, perhaps over a board game in the living room or an iced tea on the porch. Mealtime was as much about a discussion of the day's events as it was about food. Some of our oldest relatives remember those days, but it's obvious that those times are long gone.

The first obstacle to good conversation today is that most of us are at the mercy of electronic devices. There's always a TV on at home or a radio or CD playing in the car. Almost everybody carries a phone, an iPod, a Blackberry, a Bluetooth, or some other device. How often do we see two people together in a car, on the street, or even at a restaurant table, and one of them is listening to music, chatting on a cell phone, or texting someone? That is not conducive to good conversation with the person at hand, the one who deserves our attention!

The electronic devices are a symptom of our frantic pace of living. Everybody's incredibly busy and stressed out: juggling jobs, appointments, and family responsibilities; getting bombarded with screaming headlines and the pressures of a bad economy; never really being out of reach of that ring tone or the twenty-four-hour news cycle.

All of that makes it difficult for two people just to sit down, face-to-face, and let the conversation take them someplace meaningful. We come home aggravated by someone at work or in traffic or something going on in the world, and we too often take it out on the people we love. We snap at them or retreat into watching TV or using the computer.

We treasure the time we have to spend as a family, although, like most families these days, we're on the go a lot. We definitely don't have the classic dinner-table scenes you see in Norman Rockwell paintings. In fact, sometimes we wonder why we have a dining room—we never use it! We're more likely to have Eddie standing or sitting at the island in the kitchen; Eriq, our six-year-old, on the floor playing with his toys until it's time to eat, when he'll come and sit at the kitchen table; and Taj joining him when lunch or dinner is finally ready. But all through that time, we're talking about our day or what's coming up, or we're joking with each other. We know how important that sort of loving family communication is.

TALK TO ME!

People need to talk! We are social creatures. Relationships need conversation like plants need water. It's the way we learn about each other, the way we bond with each other. It's how we explore our lives and dreams. If you and your significant other aren't engaged in regular conversation, you're cheating yourself out of the best part of togetherness. And talking is the best training for a long-term relationship. Ask any couple who's managed to spend a lifetime together—good conversation definitely becomes more important than good sex as the years go by.

We need to set aside the time to talk. Each of us needs to be understood, to share our joys and sorrows, to confide in someone who can offer understanding, intimacy, and safety. That takes conversation, and conversation takes time. Yes, there will be times when we need to be alone, to regroup, but even then we need to be able to say, "I need some time by myself. Let's talk in thirty minutes."

What are we suggesting? It's simple—that couples regularly

take the time to turn off the devices and talk. It could be at home in the living room, although a park bench or a walk might be a better setting if you need help in resisting the urge to turn conversational intimacy into physical intimacy. There will be time for sex. Now is the time to remember that more relationships have been derailed by too little conversation than by too little sex. Especially early in a relationship, talk is the key to the right kind of intimacy.

I kid you not, Eddie and I used to stay on the phone literally for hours. It was a routine we had. Every night, we'd start about 7:30 and get off at about 2:00 in the morning—really! We would talk and talk and talk about everything. We'd start off with, "Hey, guy, what was your day like? How are you doing?" "Well, let me tell you what happened to me." It would just go from there—we were like girlfriends! Just the fact that he was willing to talk like that let me know I had someone special. And I had to have it. If I missed his call, my day wasn't right.

One of the most useful things we did was to argue. We would get into it sometimes, and one of us would say, "You know what? I'll just talk to you later." We'd hang up, and then about an hour later one of us would call and say, "Are you OK now?" Even when we argued about the

biggest things, we'd end up seeing that it was just a conversation and that the world hadn't come to an end. We'd work it out on the phone. Then there were the times when our conversation would make us laugh about something that we were arguing about that was just stupid. We learned that all we really needed was to talk and we could sort through anything. And we learned that by talking!
—Taj

Once we started talking, the floodgates really opened up. It didn't take any time at all. It just kind of happened. I was intrigued by her. I thought she was attractive, but then I learned how much fun she was to talk to. We had so much in common, whether it was our backgrounds or the music we liked to listen to. We shared funny stories and laughed together. Just getting to know each other made for some really good conversations. We could be silly with each other, and we could be serious. It was a really good situation. It really was. —Eddie

DEALING WITH CONFLICTS

One of the things you have to do as a couple is learn to resolve conflicts—and there are definitely going to be some. Part of the problem with those friends of ours was that they got married before they had a chance to see how they would react when they disagreed.

Seeing how you resolve conflicts is an important part of building a relationship. There's going to be trouble if one partner or the other thinks he or she is always right and is unwilling to listen to the other. And the sexes have different approaches to problem solving. We process things differently. Often, women are more likely to want to talk through a situation. Men are more likely to want to take action right away.

Couples need to learn to state and resolve their disagreements and come out the other end still friendly, still unified. It doesn't take magic. It just takes understanding, patience, and practice, all of which takes—and here comes that word again—time.

I don't like confrontation. I don't like tension. I don't like to argue all the time. It's too much energy. There would be hours or days when we were not talking to each other, and I try not to do that now. I want to move on from that. I was always the one to try to bring it back to the center. I'd say, "Let's talk about this. Let's come to common ground." I was always

hoping for the best, trying to be the one to make it move forward, because when she got mad, she'd stay that way. —Eddie

I have a tendency to be overly sensitive. Little things bother me. I knew, in coming into a relationship with Eddie, that I was going to have to figure out why. I was going to have to be able to talk about that part of myself. Otherwise, he was going to be blindsided by my emotions without knowing why they were there.

Obviously, the answers were in my background, but Eddie didn't know that at first. He didn't know that I grew up in a household filled with domestic violence. He didn't know that I was molested as a child. He didn't know that I had had physically abusive boyfriends. So if he would say, "You know what? Today I'm just going to roll with my guys. You stay here," I would take it personally. I wanted him to want to stay with me so we could do whatever it would be that day. I had to catch myself from reverting back to my old ways of thinking he obviously didn't love me, and I'm sure he would think, Geez, she's so needy. He couldn't understand why because he didn't understand the emotions that I worked with every day.

I think I was just going through a lot because my musical career was on a downswing and it was an adjustment *for me. I had to stand behind him; he was the star of our group. I literally went from Taj in SWV to Eddie George's girlfriend. That became my name—Eddie George's Girlfriend! It was hard because I knew I was worth so much more, I'd done so much more, but anything and everything I'd been through seemed to become null and void because his star was shining so bright. —Taj*

I didn't notice any of that because I was so focused on honing my craft, on making sure I could pick up a blitz on Sunday, and on enjoying my girlfriend. I didn't see it from her perspective. At that time, it was hard for me to see from *anybody's* perspective. It wasn't just about making money. I wanted to be the best. I wanted to be a legend. I had to pour my heart, my soul, my entire being into that. When I did come out of that for a brief time, I wanted to enjoy myself. I didn't have a chance to see things from her point of view. I was a superstar at the top of my game when we were dating. I knew that in a situation like ours, people are going to say things. They're going to hate on you, demean you, say you're not anything in order to lower your position or demean the relationship, just to have an edge. I guess that was what she

was going through, and I was so preoccupied with
my career that I didn't have a chance to see it.
—Eddie

LEARNING TO TRUST

Trust is as big a relationship issue as there is. Without it, true
intimacy, true bonding, is impossible. Some of us have to relearn
trust after a bad experience or two. Others, especially those who
have grown up in difficult circumstances with people who were
not always trustworthy, have to learn it for the first time.

Each of us brings a past into a relationship—old boyfriends or
girlfriends, sometimes ex-spouses. Each of us brings a different
attitude about friends of the opposite sex, about flirtation and its
boundaries. Each couple comes to its own agreements and sets its
own tone.

Like everything else we discuss in this chapter, the basis when
it comes to trust is communication. You don't have to know every
detail of every prior relationship, but it's important to know your
partner's attitudes, to understand what makes him or her tick.
That knowledge is the foundation of trust in a relationship, and
you want it to be as strong as it can be.

Communication brings knowledge. Knowledge brings trust. Trust helps overcome conflict—and all of that takes time.

She had a lot of insecurity that came from her background, and at first I didn't get it. She could get very emotional over absolutely nothing, and since there were a lot of trust issues, it could be a real strain. This was the hard part of getting to know each other. She had to learn to deal with everything we were going through. She'd be flying off the handle about things, and I was young and I didn't really understand women or people in general or myself. I didn't know what made them or me tick. It was very hard on both of us.

Still, something in me said, "She's a good girl. We can get through this. We can get to some level of understanding."

She had to learn to trust. The breakthrough I had to have was in learning not to take her for granted. I would try to find reasons not to commit, not to marry her. It was something I'd been dealing with since I'd been a freshman in college, looking at life with one woman versus life with all those women out there. And I thought she would always be there, regardless of what I did. For a

**long time I took that for granted. And I had to learn not
to. —Eddie**

Part of what we had going for us was that we were
both celebrities. I had toured the world with SWV. When
we met, he was a college athlete, and I had sold a couple
of million records. When he made it to the pros and
became a celebrity, I understood what he was going
through. Once he started his pro career, nobody said no
to him. I had to realize where his arrogance came from.
It wasn't directed toward me. It was just something he
was living. I had to sit back and let him live it. People
would say, "Why do you put up with some of the things
he does?" There was a birthday party where he asked me
to stay home and let him go celebrate. People couldn't
understand how I could handle it. I said, "My boyfriends
from the past prepared me for my husband of the future."
I could handle it and get over it. I gave him certain
allowances because I'd been there. Our jobs weren't normal, and I had to realize that. It was a case where our
celebrity helped us.

Then there was the fact that I'd been through so much
with my ex-boyfriends. If I hadn't gone through that, I
don't think I would have been prepared for the magnitude
of the Eddie George phenomenon. It would have been way

too much to handle for somebody who was as weak as I was emotionally. —Taj

A lot of the baggage I brought into our relationship came out of a playboy mentality I carried. It's something a lot of men have. It's about looking for short-term, feel-good-type things, just to stroke your ego. It could be looking for women, going to strip clubs, being flirtatious to make yourself feel good. In my case, I know it was a defense mechanism. My perception of what a relationship was still wasn't healthy. Above all, I wanted my freedom.

Then there was the fact that I knew that some of the people around me had ulterior motives. As a professional athlete, I had been burned several times. You never know what women are there for. It could be just your status or your money. And it wasn't just in relationships with women, but in professional relationships too. There was a lot of "I'll keep you at arm's length" in my approach to people, and it was that way in the beginning with Taj. —Eddie

When Eddie and I started dating, I had to learn to trust again, and that's the hardest thing to do when you've just gotten out of a terrible relationship where trust has been demolished. And it was really tough because of the circumstances. Eddie was in the thick of his career, doing all these appearances and autograph signings. He was still having fun. It's not a situation that makes trusting easy.

We didn't really set ground rules, but I think when you decide you're going to date somebody, it's an unspoken law: You don't date anybody else! You stick with me, I'll stick with you, and we'll be good. But of course that didn't always work out, and we did have tiffs about that. But one thing I will tell you, I definitely felt a sense of priority when it came to me. There was no other person I could ever pinpoint, although, like I said, he was living his life and I'm sure there were times when I couldn't find him that he wasn't just reading a book! But I couldn't explode. I had to work on that one. I had to understand I couldn't take out my frustrations from the past on him. I had to deal with the past so as not to lash out at him. One of the things I started doing was reading self-help books, doing body cleansers, trying to make myself brand new.

That's part of why I think we were so fortunate to be living in two different cities. There would have been too many issues, too many things I would not have been able to avoid emotionally, that would have sabotaged us had we been in the same city. I was terrible in my twenties. I would go crazy over nonsense. But because we were apart,

I was able to deal with myself, with my own reactions to everything, before I dealt with him. —Taj

WORKING TOGETHER: TOOLS AND EXERCISES

Just as it's important for us to look at ourselves, as we did in the first chapter, it's important for couples to learn to look together at their relationship. The approach is similar. Below are some questions designed to help you look at, discuss, and work on your relationship. As we've said, conversation is the sunlight of every relationship, and this is your chance to explore yours constructively.

This first group of questions is for you to answer separately. They're designed to get you thinking about things you'll be discussing with your partner. Some of these questions or areas of discussion will really strike a nerve. Those are the ones to focus on. This is the part where you look at yourself, by yourself. Write out your thoughts.

🦋 What attracted you to your partner?

What attracted your partner to you?

What do you have in common?

What do you bring to the relationship that's positive?

What do you bring that's negative?

What does your partner bring that's positive?

What does your partner bring that's negative?

❧ What do you and your partner laugh about?

❧ What do you argue about?

❧ Do you agree on the best way to settle disagreements?

❧ What makes you happiest about your partner?

❧ What makes you angriest or most uncomfortable about your partner?

❧ Can you talk about pretty much anything?

❦ Have you talked about children? vacations? dreams? where to live?

❦ What subjects don't you talk about?

❦ What do your friends think of your partner?

❦ Does your partner get along with your family?

❦ Do you get along with your partner's family?

❦ Do family and friends think you and your partner make a good couple?

❧ When you talk about your partner to your friends or family, do you withhold information you think might make him or her look bad?

❧ Do you generally keep your emotions under control with your partner?

❧ Does your partner keep them under control around you?

❧ If you're not married, have you had sex yet?

❧ If so, did you feel ready?

🦋 Were both of you comfortable with your decision?

🦋 Are both of you still comfortable with it?

🦋 What are your favorite things to do together?

🦋 Do you both get enough "alone" time? Do you get too much?

That's a lot to digest about yourself and your relationship. Think about the picture you've painted by answering these questions. Is it a good, positive picture? Does it sound like you have a healthy relationship? If not, why not?

Let's think about the process of meditation as it relates to an exercise like this. Find a place where you can be alone for an hour or so. Spend quiet, quality time with God. Then give thought to your relationship. Listen for what God might be telling you about it.

Now it's time to talk with your partner. Below is another group of questions. They provide sort of a grown-up version of Truth or Dare or *The Newlywed Game*. In this case, though, it's not about being titillating. It's not about feeling embarrassed. It's about looking at your differences and looking for ways to resolve them—by coming to an agreement, by reaching a compromise, or by agreeing to disagree. It's also about looking for common ground, about acknowledging all those areas where you're in agreement.

You'll see that some of these questions are the same ones you sorted through by yourself. There, they helped you look at your side of the story. Now you'll be looking at how your viewpoint compares with your partner's. Every partnership is comprised of two individuals, each with a point of view. The trick in a successful relationship is knowing how to bring those two points of view together. This exercise will help you learn to do that.

This time, there won't be any writing since you've already written your answers to the set of questions above. Remember, you're trying to learn about yourselves as a couple and improve your relationship. Keep the discussion respectful and helpful. You might begin and end with a prayer so you're aligned with the fact that God is the cornerstone of your partnership. One of those we're fond of is Matthew 6:33 (CEB): "Desire first and foremost God's kingdom and God's righteousness, and all these things will be given to you as well."

❧ What attracted you to each other?

❧ What do you have in common?

❧ What's your favorite way to spend time together?

❧ When there's a difference of opinion about what to do or how to spend time, whose opinion generally prevails?

❧ Do both of you feel comfortable with that?

❧ What do you argue about?

🦋 What do you laugh about?

🦋 Do your friends like you as a couple?

🦋 Do you get along with each other's families?

🦋 Each of you describe your partner to your partner as though you were describing him or her to a friend. Talk about your description.

🦋 If you're not married, have you had sex yet?

🦋 If so, did you feel ready?

🦋 Were both of you comfortable with your decision?

🦋 Are both of you still comfortable with it?

🦋 Do you both get enough "alone" time? Do you get too much?

If you're in counseling of some sort together, these questions might provide subject areas for upcoming sessions. If not, they'll form the basis for discussions that may well be useful and that you may want to revisit from time to time.

Conversations like these can provide an ongoing pathway to the kind of intimacy that couples often don't get enough of—knowledge of and comfort with each other.

Now it's time to move on to specific areas that often cause trouble for couples.

CHAPTER THREE

LIVE BY FAITH

With this chapter, we start to deal in depth with the issues at the core of a marriage—faith, money, and sex. We begin with faith because we can't imagine a partnership with anything else as the foundation. A couple who builds a life and relationship on biblical foundations can work through almost any conflict. As we like to say, "A faith-filled heart is a happy heart." One of the great early surprises in our relationship was realizing we could talk about our faith. It gave us something to use as the basis for everything else and is one of the main reasons we've been successful as a couple through the years.

A strong faith foundation goes a long way in any relationship. Many people go through life wondering why they find themselves in bad situations. All relationships have problems, but where there is a lack of faith, those problems seem to grow much faster.

As individuals and as couples, all of us are going to face adversity. There will be times when we will have to rely on something or somebody bigger than we are. For us, the answer lies in our spirituality, in our relationship with God. That doesn't mean we're perfect or that we're praying every hour of every day. It does mean that seeking God's will and guidance is built into the way we live our lives day to day. It allows us to get centered. That's why we're spending this chapter exploring the role of faith in our lives and in our relationship, and looking at techniques for making the best use of faith and meditation as a couple.

After the breakup with my ex-boyfriend, I knew I needed to work on me—just me. I decided I was done with guys. I thought, I am my biggest weakness. I keep looking toward these men to be mother and father, to be the family I always wanted. *I was grabbing at anybody. I had no criteria. You just had to be tall, and I had to think (not even* believe, *just* think!) *you loved me back—or hope that you loved me back.*

Since I had decided I was going to go this road alone, I wanted to be spiritually prepared, so I started reading the Bible. I actually started with Revelation because I wanted to know what was going to happen in the future so I could be prepared for it. I was hoping that whatever would happen would happen soon so I wouldn't have to deal with my pain any longer. I would read every night, and I literally almost made it through the entire Bible. Every day as I read I would just sit there and think about everything I had done wrong, everything that had ever happened to me, everything that my family had ever done to me. I kept saying, "I'm tired of being everybody's victim."

I had always felt that because my family had split up and I was on my own, I didn't have room for error. I had to be the best person I could possibly be because if I was good and nice and perfect, other people would be good and nice and perfect to me too.

Of course, it wasn't like that. Life never is. I came to realize that everything and everyone is a work in progress. I may have had renewed faith, but not everyone was going to have the same faith I had. They didn't have access to the same strength. I still believed God was going to repair me as long as I worked at it, but everyone else wasn't going to be on the same page.

As I worked even harder on myself, I began to try to meditate. I would get up at 8:00 a.m. and meditate for a few minutes. I wasn't very good at it. I prefer a good old-fashioned prayer; it's all the same to me. Afterward, I would go to the gym for two or three hours. I felt that if I could work out and stay physically healthy, I could stay mentally strong.

While I was doing all this, asking God to help me work on me, the last thing on my mind was another boyfriend. I knew I could not start that cycle again. But the next thing I knew, there were several people approaching me for relationships. I felt as though I was auditioning someone for a new role. That role? The rest of my life! I turned them all down. I was like, "No, I'll go out and sit down and eat with you," but I just shut down emotionally as far as having a boyfriend was concerned. I knew if I did involve myself with another guy, I would get off that path of self-sufficiency I was trying to get on.

I started going to a prophetic church, and I remember talking with the pastor, who said, "Stay on your path. God has a plan for you. Someone is coming your way." I'm like, "What? No! Not again! I don't want that! I just want to work on me and get me right because I'm tired of having people walk all over my heart."

I dug into my faith in a way I never had before. I had grown up in a small Baptist church in Brooklyn, but I had never really cared for it. My family went there, but to me it was boring. I also felt like the people who ran the church weren't very holy. I didn't see a good example there, so I didn't lock into it. That left me with a religious foundation that wasn't very strong. Just how weak it was became clear when my then-boyfriend and I broke up, because I was a wreck by that time!

I believe if I'd had a stronger faith then, I wouldn't have been in the situation I was in. I didn't have anything firm under my feet. I was looking for a foundation where there was none. But now my faith became my new foundation. It became my strong-heeled shoes that allowed me to stand up and keep my posture straight while I kept moving.

I won't say that walking in faith wasn't tough, because while you're trying to believe in God, you will have all kinds of situations coming at you to tell you, "Oh, it's not going to work. God doesn't exist!" But you have to continue to believe and keep that faith and know that whatever you're going through, it's for a reason, and that reason is to make you stronger and prepare you for something else.

And if I hadn't had the sense to turn to God when I did, my relationship with Eddie might not have worked. I wouldn't have been ready. Again, just to be clear, I wasn't in church twenty-four hours a day, and I never tell people they have to do that. I didn't go to Bible studies. I didn't go to church every day. I went every Sunday. That was my God Day, the day I spent in my deepest meditation modes. After church, I had my candles going and my gospel music playing, just feeling the presence of the Lord in my spirit. I just knew that God was going to take me through whatever I was facing, and he did.

What I do ask people is, "How is your faith?" I definitely believe that if you have the slightest faith, the faith of a mustard seed, you can get through anything. And there was plenty for me to get through. There was all of the residue from my childhood and past relationships, and I still had my doubts. I had a mentor, Denise Baize, a minister from the Bronx. She was my spiritual advisor. She would talk to me when I was questioning myself, wondering whether I was doing the right things and whether I was following the path I was supposed to. She would assure me that God was there for me. She'd say, "It's rough now, but every time you get cut there's a healing process that takes *place. Your wound may itch and be sore, but eventually it heals and you don't even see it anymore. That's what's happening to you. You're going through this healing process, and it's going to be tough for you at times. Just stay on the path, and you'll look back and one day you'll say, 'Gosh, I can't believe I went through that.'" And she was right! I look back now, and I can't believe I went through that! —Taj*

I had a pretty diverse background in terms of faith and religion. My grandmother was born Catholic and I went to Catholic schools, but I grew up in the Baptist Church. I'd call it a strong background, since any black family you know will know how to talk to God, and mine was no exception.

After two years of high school, I went to Fork Union Military Academy, a faith-based Christian school. Faith wasn't just something you dealt with in chapel. It touched every aspect of your life. The school was tough, and faith helped keep me going. I dreamed of playing football on the college and pro levels. Actually, *dreamed* is too mild a word. I was *consumed* with it, although there were plenty of times when it didn't seem to be working.

Music helped keep my spirits up, and I think its

uplifting power fed into my faith. One big example came from my Uncle Kevin. He was a real father figure. He and my Uncle Derrick were really into sports, and they helped me learn to set goals. Uncle Kevin showed me the basics of weight lifting, and he made a tape for me that really helped keep me going in high school. It was a tape of MC Hammer's "U Can't Touch This." Kevin changed the lyrics and rapped over it. The tape painted a picture of me as an untouchable running back. He also had Al Jarreau's song "Could You Believe" on it, making the point that I could be the best if I would just believe. I listened to that tape every single night. I wasn't starting at the time. I wasn't playing much at all my junior year, but I was able to keep looking forward. Nothing was going very well, but I had enough faith and enough reinforcement from my Uncle Kevin that I was able to keep working my tail off.

During my senior year, I started, and I rushed for thirteen hundred yards and scored twenty-two touchdowns. At the end of the year, though, I had exactly zero scholarship offers. None. But I wasn't going to let that dream die. I went into the coach's office every afternoon from 3:30 to 5:30 and called every college, in alphabetical order, to have our athletic director tell them about me and to ask about me coming to their school as a walk-on. I had 101 schools turn me down. It was devastating. I didn't know what I was going to do.

I remember praying, trying to find the way: "God, you gave me the dream to be a football player. It's so strong in me, but I don't see physically how it's going to happen. Today no one wants me. I'm not on anybody's radar. How is this going to work?"

Finally, I decided to stay in high school an extra year. Fork Union had a postgraduate program, so I got myself together. I drew on every ounce of faith and determination I had, but even then, I believed that faith has to be accompanied by action. I worked out, built up my body, built up my speed, and became a different person, a different player, by the time my fifth year of high school came around. I had a great year, and this time I earned the attention of the major Division I schools. The scholarship offers came in, and I accepted one from Ohio State.

I may have achieved that part of the dream, but there were even bigger difficulties to come. I scored five touchdowns early my freshman year at OSU, but then after two fumbles in the Illinois game, I played very little the rest of that year or in my sophomore year.

I had dreamed of being a Heisman Trophy winner, but I spent two years mostly on the bench. I wanted to leave school. I had to draw on every ounce of faith I had to keep going. Finally, in my junior year, I got the chance to start. I had two great years at Ohio

State and achieved my dream of winning the Heisman Trophy my senior year. —Eddie

FROM TWO TO ONE

There comes a point at which the faith of two individuals becomes the combined faith of a couple. What has been two singular approaches to God becomes a partnership that then places God at the helm. This is the backdrop for the partnership we looked at with the questions at the end of the last chapter. This is what gives that partnership its importance, its spiritual aspect. The walk of two people together with God sanctifies the big and small things we might otherwise overlook or take for granted. It gives the day-to-day life an eternal significance.

Eddie and I used to talk a lot about faith and religion. Of course, we were talking a lot about everything. Fortunately, by the time we started dating, I had already been focusing on what I needed to do for myself. That

meant for once that I wasn't completely attaching to the man in my life. I allowed myself to get to know him instead of being in love with him from the moment he said hello. And the fact that I was taking my spiritual life seriously made for a better me, and it helped a lot when it was time for us to get on the same page spiritually.

I was still working with Denise as my spiritual advisor, and I would have her talk to Eddie. He was having trouble sleeping, and I guess there were things that just really bothered him, things that he wasn't talking about, that he was just dealing with. Of course, I had no idea. So, Denise would talk to him, and she would pray with him, which got him more into it and reinforced his spiritual side. He really started to get into the word. He would read the Bible a lot, and we would discuss it sometimes. We would have our own Bible-study sessions together. It was just really good. I felt like I was a positive influence on him and his life, and I think it brought us closer. For the first time in my life I actually felt like someone was attaching to me and needed me. Finally!

This was an unorthodox way of growing together spiritually because a lot of times we were doing it long distance. We'd be on the phone talking, and I'd mention Jesus and that would start up a conversation that would last for hours. But it worked. We would go to church together, which is something I had never done with any of my boyfriends, ever! I had never discussed religion or the Bible with them. For Eddie not to shy away from the person I *was spiritually felt really different for me. Our relationship was rooted in spirituality, and it felt wonderful. It attached me to him in a way that wasn't unhealthy, which had never been the case in my other relationships. It gave me a way to attach that wasn't needy or childlike.*

Being in a relationship with a spiritual center helps give you a moral sense. It lets you know right from wrong. It helps you sort out the things you should and should not be doing. It erases a lot of the bull. And it helped us grow.
—Taj

When we knew we were heading toward marriage and a family, we started counseling through the church. We really wanted ours to be a strong foundation, and we felt that if we could get God at the center of our relationship, we could get through everything, good and bad.

Our first sessions, with the Elder Barry Towles, gave us a chance to open up and talk about our backgrounds, our hopes and fears, and our feelings about each other. They helped us learn to pray for each other when we were apart and to keep each other encouraged, to have each other's back no matter what. Those sessions really brought us close together and helped us grow on a spiritual level.

**Going to church while we were dating was impor-
tant for us. It helped keep us in the word. Altogether,
our faith gave us a bigger vision than we might have
had otherwise. It taught us not to take the good times
for granted, and it taught us that when things go bad,
it's not the end. It's not the time to quit. Bad times are
just part of the process. Having faith means you're
willing to work through them, to look for common
ground, to give and take, knowing there's a solution
somewhere up ahead.**

**Just like faith helped keep me going when I was
struggling as an athlete, faith helped Taj and me keep
going as a couple. It's been really important for us
since the beginning. —Eddie**

FAITH AND FOOTWORK

Faith is not just about those moments when we're in prayer. It
encompasses everything we do. It's not just hoping for the best. It
involves studying and reading the Bible to learn more about
God's plan. Faith is not just blind hope. It is, Paul tells us, "the
reality of what we hope for, the proof of what we don't see"
(Hebrews 11:1 CEB).

In our own lives, looking at our actions and attitudes will help us as we look toward the future. Sometimes it will mean revisiting our assumptions, questioning our motives, and adjusting our paths. That's why the questions we answered in chapters 1 and 2 are part of a faithful walk. We can't expect the best outcomes unless we are willing to do the footwork. God moves the mountains. It's up to us to pack shovels.

There was a point in our relationship when I thought I might have made a mistake. Eddie and I had been dating long distance for four years, and then we decided to take our relationship closer. I moved to Nashville to attend Belmont University, so we were finally in the same city. We were together a lot more, and it seemed that the closer we became, the less his family seemed to like it. They weren't exactly welcoming, and all I heard from him was, "Just ignore it." And I realized I was still just a girlfriend.

As I learned more about his good and bad points, I noticed how much my big, strong, wonderful boyfriend was a kid at heart. That drove me crazy because it seemed to me that he had never really grown up. He was having the time of his life, and he was stuck in his twenties even after he reached his thirties.

So in my mind I had to decide, Am I going to go

forward with this, or am I going to worry more about my emotions? *I think a part of me was just a little selfish because I was considering my needs and wants. At that point I didn't have any kids, I didn't have an engagement ring, and there were no plans for us to be married, so I had no reason to think of us as a "couple" couple, a long-term couple. I was thinking,* This is just fun to him, and I'm not looking just for fun anymore. I'm looking for something more concrete.

I was second-guessing it, and all I could think was, Go back into you. Go back into working on and fixing you. Separate yourself again, and then move on because obviously this is not what you thought it was. If it was, it would have been perfect, and all of this would not have happened.

I started to think that maybe I had been reading the signs wrong. Even though we had a spiritual connection, maybe Eddie wasn't supposed to be "the one" or my husband. Maybe we were just supposed to be really good friends. Maybe he was just supposed to be there to help me through this period where I was trying to move forward. I started to second-guess my newfound strength. Here I go again, *I thought,* looking for something that's not there.

That's when I decided to leave, something I talked about in chapter 1. I had a year of school left, and I made plans to pack up everything and go back home to New York. I was just going to start my life afresh and move forward from there. I wanted to get everything about me lined up so I could be this wonderful, mature adult. I was ready to move forward, and I didn't think that "my husband" was.

I guess your actions definitely speak louder than your words. I think he noticed that something had changed, and it caused him to change. He may have sensed that I was pulling back, and I think the situation helped him follow me as opposed to walking away from me. Before I could even put my plans into place, he surprised me with that engagement ring and told me that he cared more about my emotions than he cared about himself and that he didn't want to see me unhappy.

I didn't have to tell him. My actions had expressed it, but it wasn't a matter of slamming things. It wasn't arguing all day. It was me taking care of me. It taught me that once you consider you and get you right, everything else will fall into place. —Taj

LIVING IN FAITH

At first, Adam and Eve were complete people, both in the sense that they hadn't sinned yet and in the sense that each possessed the proper unity of body and spirit. We are designed to be complete in that same way, and it's our understanding of a life in God's will that it takes into account body as well as mind.

For us, living in faith means getting to the core of our life purpose through God. It begins with prayer and Bible study, but it extends into every aspect of our lives.

Living in faith means respecting God's creation, which includes us. It means caring for our bodies with good food, vitamins, exercise, and relaxation. All of the things that make us better physically can make us better spiritually if we go into them with the right mind-set.

Our bodies function best given the proper nutrition. We can see what a diet of junk food and inactivity is doing to us as a nation physically. It's not much of a leap to realize that those things have a profound mental and spiritual effect as well. Is it difficult to imagine that those things contribute to depression and a lack of energy? Body, mind, and spirit are interconnected, and since we are instructed to look at our bodies as God's temples, we should treat them as such.

We know that exercise contributes to health and strength, and we know it contributes to a feeling of well-being. Lifting weights, running, walking, doing aerobics, playing golf—there are a lot of ways to make exercise part of our lives. Most of them have the added benefit of taking us out of our day, giving us the chance to be alone in our thoughts with God. And the healthy burn that comes with getting the heart pumping and working up a sweat is a good way to work out negative emotions. That means exercise can be a great stress reliever, and there's no overstating the importance of that.

Heart disease and diabetes are listed as among the major killers in our society, but too often they're only symptoms. The major killer behind so many modern ailments is stress. Stress takes you out of your natural balance of body and spirit. It depletes you of energy. It makes you prone to depression. Those things stand in the way of your relationship with God, and that can't help but have a negative impact on your relationship with your partner.

Staying fit gave us a little more time to laugh and enjoy each other. I have never been athletic, but I love to work out. I knew that there was no way I could keep up with Eddie's workout regimen, but I had a ton of fun trying. Whenever we would work out together, I could complain and sulk, and in turn he could console and encourage me. We would have so much fun going back and forth with our playful banter. Whenever we were in Los Angeles, we would hit the stairs in Santa Monica or walk along the beach. I would be miserable working with his yoga instruc-tor, and he would be patronizing when he joined me with my workout tapes. Nevertheless, we were together and enjoying a healthy life. Nowadays, with our kids and work

schedules, it's harder to do some of the fun things we used to do together all the time. OK, it's harder for me! Eddie is diligent with his regimen. I could be in labor, and as long as the baby's not crowning, he'll be on a treadmill or doing push-ups! The man is serious about his workout! —Taj

MEDITATION

Speaking of stress relief, one of the greatest means we've found is meditation. Once our prayer life is in order and we're eating right and exercising, meditation is one of the most useful things we can do. It's a way for us to get past the jumble of thoughts in our heads to a place where we can just *be*, able to feel and acknowledge God's presence within and around us.

For most of us, our thoughts simply swirl around as day after frantic day unfolds. We never seem to slow down enough to sort through the chaos. As we meditate, getting still, becoming quiet, we can learn to let those thoughts settle down as well. Meditation opens creative space in our minds so that we start to feel the answers to our questions. It's a practice we have made a welcome part of our lives. We'll talk below about how we do it and how you can too.

Then there is another aspect of life that many of us overlook. It's important to take time to laugh. It's both a stress reliever and a way to keep things in perspective. As tough as the world can be, we weren't meant to be downhearted. The two of us are always cracking up over silly things, from TV shows to the things the kids say and do. We think it brings us closer to each other—and to God.

The process of being complete has a lot of elements. We are complex creatures. But it's possible to tie all those aspects together into a unified whole, to combine our bodies and spirits in a way that lets us live fully in faith.

So much of what I do is designed to keep me in touch with God, to put me on a spiritual level. I could list all kinds of things—praying, meditating, working out, walking the dogs, playing golf, talking and laughing with Taj, being outside enjoying nature. It's all connected if I look at it right. Everything I do can be an opportunity for me to feel God's spirit. That's important to me, to try to be in constant connection. It's how I've gotten this far in my life.

It was definitely part of how I was able to accomplish so much as a football player. I attribute my

success there to the preparation of my body and the dedication of my spirit. There were days when I played hurt, when I played sore, when I wasn't really into it, but then as now I asked the Spirit to guide me, asked God to take my head out of it and to let me rely on my instrument.

You work on the intangibles, on your skill set. In my case, I worked on balance, on my cutting ability, on my strength and endurance. But at some point, your inner spirit has to take over. You run possessed, allowing God's spirit to fill you, allowing that artistic flow within you as an athlete to come out. You've done the work to put all the components in place, and when the moment of truth comes, you rely on what amounts to intuition and feel to guide you.

In my personal life, the skill set is all the things I do to work on myself and on our relationship, using the tools and ideas we're talking about in this book. In my professional life, it's things like going to business school, taking acting classes, and doing all the other things I do to improve my knowledge and my talents. And in the morning I ask God's spirit to guide me on both fronts.

My morning prayer begins with me acknowledging God for letting me see another day. I express my gratitude and ask for the power and ability to be productive and to be a blessing to others. Prayer is my rock. It keeps me strong, which is vital, because adversity and stress will definitely come. There's no way around them. The question is, *How do you deal with that stress?*

I've learned that it's not really mine to deal with. My job is to do footwork. On a day-to-day level, I do my work, hone my skills, perfect my craft. The results are up to God. If I do what I've been given the ability to do, everything will go as God wants it. When it comes to stress and adversity, my job is to show up in prayer and meditation and to let it all go. It's not mine. It's God's.

The hour in the morning that I devote to meditation and yoga is my time of devotion, my time of stillness. It's my starting point, my way to get grounded. Prayer is the way I speak to God. Meditation is where God speaks to me. I seek his guidance, opening up every part of my being—physical, mental, emotional—to set my intentions and my focus for the day. I need that in the morning, and I need to tap in to that throughout the day. When I leave my meditation space, I want to carry that feeling into every phase of my life. I'm in communication with God, trying to reach that place where I'm not living for self but where I'm seeking his will rather than my own.

Sometimes my schedule, especially with the traveling I do, can get in the way, but I always come back to meditation as home base. It's designed to remind me that God is my life force, the breath, the spirit that

**drives me. His presence is tied in to my identity and
well-being. It is the thing that lets me understand my
life purpose and gives me the strength to pursue it.
—Eddie**

*Eddie is a meditator. He is in his meditation chair every
morning, and he's tried to teach me how to get to that place
of peace, but I have to admit that once we're up in the
morning, I get too busy with Eriq and the dog and the
house and my schedule to sit and meditate very often.*

*I am more of a pray-er. Throughout the day, I'll find lit-
tle moments to stop and think, to thank God for the blessings he's given me. In fact, about a year ago I decided I
wasn't going to pray for anything specific anymore because
he has given me so much. I feel guilty getting on my knees
and telling God what I need or want, so I just thank him for
the gifts of my children and of my health. Especially after
competing on* Survivor, *I feel so blessed to have all of the
people and "things" that I have in my life. From the time I
was a little girl, I've always wanted a house with a little
white picket fence, a husband, two kids, and a dog. I have
two beautiful kids. I have two dogs. I have a wonderful husband. I don't have my picket fence, but I have a gated com-
munity! I never lose sight of how blessed we are.*

My morning prayer time includes a little Bible reading,

and it's a sign of the times that I do it with verses sent to my iPhone! A lot of times I'll catch myself saying, "Ooh, I've gotta save that one!" It shows me that everything—even modern electronic gadgets—can be part of my spiritual life.

As a family, our daily walk of faith starts with saying grace. It's a way to get our kids into a conscious acknowledgment of God as a presence in our lives. The whole family takes turns saying the grace. It's not a long, drawn-out prayer. It's something simple, like, "Strengthen our family. Make us whole. Thank you for the food as nourishment for our bodies so that we can continue to grow." Our six-year-old is not as eloquent with his grace yet, but I so enjoy listening to him. We all do. It's meant to draw all of us together. —Taj

I can honestly say that given our schedules and our travel, we don't get to eat enough meals together as a family, but when we do get to the table together, we pray. We usually take turns saying the grace. We get a kick out of listening to Eriq. You can always tell when he's hungry. His grace tends to be short and sweet.

There's more than just mealtime prayer to setting an example for Eriq. When I'm waking up in the morning or going to bed at night and he is up, I'll pray out

loud. I want him to hear me, to understand that I'm in prayer, talking to God. It's the same thing when I'm doing my morning meditation. He's welcome to come in. I want him to see the practice, to see that I have a spiritual well to tap into. That's so important. He's very sensitive to that sort of thing. I want both my sons to understand my reliance on God, on the Bible, on Jesus. I want them to see that that's the starting point in my life. —Eddie

FAITH IN ACTION

Our lives are not compartmentalized. This book is divided into chapters so we can deal with issues one at a time. But life is a jumble! We can't separate faith from action any more than we can separate money from running a household. The bricks and mortar that make up a relationship, a marriage, a household, a family, are laid on top of that faith foundation, which means how straight and strong each one is depends on the strength of that foundation.

The connection Eddie and I have spiritually is something that can be expressed and reinforced physically. As a couple, every hug, every look, every moment together can be a recognition of and celebration of the fact that you are a union. That's an extension of meditation. These days, time is such a precious commodity that it can be tough to get time together. Make every encounter count! Ten minutes on the sofa with his arm around you can be a form of meditation. You're together; you're focusing on each other; you're in that quiet place just being together. If your better half is at the stove cooking, coming in the door, or standing and talking on the phone, take a moment just to stop for a hug and to say, "I love you." Inhale each other's presence and the presence of God that fills both of you. You'd be surprised how different you can feel as you walk away to go back to what you were doing. —Taj

COUNSELING

We've talked again and again about how important conversation is, and it's absolutely vital to a relationship lived within a framework of faith. In earlier chapters, we've listed questions you can answer together as a starting point for conversation that is designed to let you see just where you are, as individuals and as a couple. We'll have some more, dealing with faith, in just a bit.

Sometimes one-on-one conversation just won't break through a problem or a standoff. We've used structured conversation in the form of counseling throughout our relationship. It started when we were dating and continues to this day, although it's changed a great deal along the way, since dating and marriage are incredibly different.

Going into counseling takes its own form of faith. It's a big step, and some people aren't willing to take it. We're willing to use counseling as a tool because we think it's helpful and because we want more than anything to succeed as a couple. It's that simple. We open ourselves up to outside opinions and outside guidance when it seems appropriate.

A lot of people would look at our backgrounds—broken homes, divorced parents, abuse, and all the other challenges we've faced—and assume that we were doomed to failure. We all know what the divorce statistics are like. But we don't want to be a statistic. We want to remain a loving and committed couple. We know that takes work and faith, and sometimes faith means bringing a trained third party into the picture. Maybe you think bringing in a third party is beneath you. Only you can decide that. But we've seen, in our own case and in the cases of many people we know, that getting help takes real bravery. Too many people with backgrounds like ours are standing amid the wreckage of relationship after relationship. We'd rather do what it takes to stay together.

We face the same challenges, the same roadblocks, the same standoffs as other people, but we're working through them. The fact that we always come out the other side is what made us real-ize we had something to share about earning—and that's what it is—a successful relationship.

Before we were married, we talked to a female pastor and a male pastor to help us address both sides of the rela-tionship. We had both come from broken households. My mother passed away when I was fourteen years old, and I had never witnessed a healthy relationship. My future hus-band's dad left when he was a child, leaving him with a void. I needed someone to tell me what I was expected to do, what the life of a wife should look like, and no man could tell me that. It was about uncovering layers in the relationship by uncovering layers in ourselves. Then, at the actual ceremony, both of them were present, and both married us. —Taj

I recommend premarital counseling and then mari-tal counseling every two years. Things change that

often. The way I think now at thirty-eight isn't the way I was thinking at thirty-five or thirty-three or thirty-one. I'm a totally different man with different life experiences. I've gone through a lot of changes in my career and in my life. My perspective is different. I'm older and wiser now. For me, it's essential to check in every once in a while to see what's resonating with me and what's resonating with her. You need the chance to explore where you are, to go in depth about things when times are good and when they're bad.

Delving deeper into your past and into your psyche, dealing with the so-called demons, changes you for the better. As you change, and as you communicate that change to your partner, your relationship changes.

It's important to continue to move, to nurture and develop your relationship as your individual lives change. Counseling has always helped us do that. — Eddie

Probably the biggest blowup we've had involved a woman with medical problems who came to Eddie for help and support. Ultimately, I thought she did not have my interests as his spouse utmost in her mind, and I thought that because of his big heart, he was being a little too naive

about what I saw as her ulterior motives. He and I were face-to-face in our disagreements about the situation. I can be pretty strong-willed, especially when I see someone trying to infiltrate my marriage. It was one of those times when we just couldn't see each other's side. Finally, he called the pastor of our church, who set up spiritual counseling that amounted to mediation between us. It was a situation where someone else was acting almost as a translator, restating each of our cases and helping us see them from a third-party perspective. When you hear your partner's point of view from someone else, it can be easier to see things more clearly. It gives you the chance to listen, to think, to chew on the information and digest it a little better. Eventually I came down off my anger, and we were able to come to an agreement and go on. Sometimes, that's what it takes. —Taj

A FOUNDATION OF FAITH: TOOLS AND EXERCISES

This group of questions is designed to help you look at your relationship within a framework of faith—and as we've discussed, many elements come under that heading.

THE SPIRITUAL

❧ Do you feel that your relationship is grounded in faith?

❧ How does that faith manifest itself?

❧ Does it draw you together?

❧ Does it give you a common vision?

❧ Do you worship together?

❧ Do you read the Bible? Alone or together?

🦋 Do you discuss what you've read?

🦋 Do you pray at the table?

🦋 Do you pray in the morning and at night?

🦋 Do you pray together or separately?

🦋 If you pray separately, have you thought about praying together?

🦋 If you have children, do you include them in your prayer?

One useful exercise involves talking about your prayer life. If every other aspect of your life is worth a little analysis, why not this one? Set aside some time to talk about how you pray, separately and together. Share your thoughts and encourage each other. It's also worth changing things up as you look for ways to improve the three-way conversation the two of you have with God. Pray somewhere you haven't prayed before—maybe in the car or in bed together. Just as variety can spice up romance, it just might bring fresh perspective to your prayer life.

THE PHYSICAL

🦋 Are you taking care of your body?

🦋 Are you at a healthy weight?

🦋 Do you eat balanced meals?

❦ Do you exercise?

❦ Do you smoke, drink, or take drugs?

❦ Do you relax (and we don't just mean watching television)?

❦ When you do watch TV or read, is the subject matter educational or uplifting?

❦ Have you tried formal meditation or at least set aside a quiet time to reflect?

Here again, make sure you're talking about health. It's hard to avoid the topic in the media, whether it's a magazine item about junk foods or a reality show about weight loss. Anything could be a springboard to a positive, mutually supportive conversation. Look for healthy additions to downtime or vacations. Talk about a visit to the nearest farmer's market for fresh produce. Have the kind of talk about meal and exercise planning that you have about planning your finances. For couples, the first step on the road to positive change is just a conversation away.

CHAPTER FOUR

HANDLE YOUR MONEY

The love of money may be the root of all evil, but money all by its lonesome is the root of plenty of the world's marital troubles. It's definitely one of the things couples argue about most.

In this chapter we'll look at our own attitudes when it comes to money, then look at ways to help make sure you've got your head straight about it.

Let's start by considering what money is. It doesn't have value on its own—it's only valuable if you can use it to buy things that do have value. So it's actually a symbol of wealth rather than wealth itself. It's a tool, something you use in order to maintain a home in the ways that love doesn't. It's how you build or buy a house, keep the lights and heat on, furnish your home, and purchase things like education and recreation. The family runs on love. Money just gives the love a place to happen and things to do.

There are plenty of ways for that simple approach to go wrong. We know that there are a lot more financial pressures on families today than at almost any time in America's history. Even during the Depression, which was far worse than what's going on now, people didn't seem to be stressed out like they are today. Most people in most parts of the country were poor, but they seemed a little better able to deal with it. It was definitely a stressful time for Americans, but those who suffered through the Depression didn't have half the modern-day goodies that we have grown attached to.

Nowadays, both people in a marriage usually work just to make ends meet. This can definitely contribute to tension in relationships. People are working longer hours and scrambling to find good day care. They're juggling errands and car pools and doctor visits and shopping trips and hoping to squeeze in a little free time.

Then, let's face it, far too many people violate the most basic economic rule—they spend more than they make! Credit card debt, mortgages taken out for primary or secondary homes, expensive vacations, big-ticket items purchased just to impress or keep up with other people—all of them have been known to shipwreck families financially. Even on a modest scale, these things can increase the tension in a household and place incredible strain on a relationship.

The bottom line, we think, is that you should handle your money—it should not handle you. It should not rule you as individuals or as a couple. It should not divide you. If the basis of your relationship lies in faith, you will have a big head start in putting finances in their proper place. Circumstances will arise that you may not have control over. Let's focus on the circumstances you do have control over.

When I was a kid, money was something that was unattainable. We just didn't have it. There were many times when I couldn't go on school trips if there was a fee involved. My brothers and I never thought about what we'd do with a million dollars because that was just outside our reality.

That's why it's crazy now to look at how things turned out for us, at what we've been blessed to have. It makes me realize that if we were to lose everything tomorrow, it would be uncomfortable, but it wouldn't be unbearable because I can reach back into my past and see that when we didn't have any money, we made it regardless. You can learn to get comfortable in your less-than situation. I'm here today, so it couldn't have been that bad.

When my mother died and I moved in with my cousin, the bills were always paid. Emotionally, those years were awful, but at least my cousin could handle her money.

While I was in high school, I dreamed of going to Howard University. It was the school you saw in all the movies, and it seemed like the perfect place to go to college.

I was thinking about law school, and Howard had one. In my senior year, my grandmother asked where I wanted to go to school.

"Howard University!" I told her.

"Well," she said, "I guess you don't want to go to college."

It was crushing. I didn't have any money, and the only people who could help at all financially were telling me they weren't going to help with a school that expensive. So I put that dream aside and applied to local colleges, figuring that with a student loan and some financial aid I would be able to afford in-state resident tuition. I applied to Baruch College, part of the City University of New York. I was accepted and received the financial aid I applied for.

Graduating from high school was like getting out of prison. The first thing I discovered about college was that they didn't send a note home if you failed to show up to class. It was up to you! You were supposed to be a responsible adult and make it to class on your own.

The second thing I discovered was that my financial aid package was so good I had all kinds of money left over. There I was, eighteen, with all the freedom I could ask for and a big wad of cash. I was almost never in class, and when I was, I still wasn't, if you know what I mean. I was a horrible student. In my first three semesters of college, I accumulated a whopping 1.7 GPA.

By the grace of God, I got into this musical group that took off, and I didn't have to deal with school anymore.

Taj (age 5)

Eddie (age 3)

Eddie in high school

Taj, Gail Aaron, and
Maisha Obey at prom

Eddie (age 15)

Taj in high school

Eddie at The Ohio
State University

Taj on stage
photography by SEVEN

Eddie with the
Heisman Trophy
totalprosports.com

Son Jaire with plaque of Eddie

Wedding day
photo by Stefanie Jasper
and Paul Sky

Taj, Jaire, and
Eddie at wedding
photo by Stefanie Jasper
and Paul Sky

Reality TV
promotion
photo © Erick Anderson

I Married A Baller

Taj receives her BA
from Belmont University

photo © Erick Anderson

Eddie, Taj, Jaire, and Eriq
at Eddie's graduation
from Kellogg School
of Management

Taj on *Survivor*

Sandy Burgin, Taj, Carolina
Eastwood, and Sydney
Wheeler from *Survivor*

LeLee, Coko,
and Taj of SWV
photo © Derek Blanks

Eddie at the helm

Eddie and sons

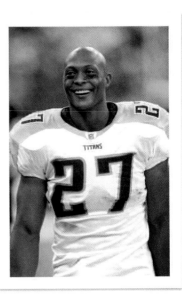

Titan Eddie
photo by Donn Jones, official
photographer of the Tennessee Titans
donnjonesphotography.com

The George family

photo © A Private Gathering Photography

Taj, Eddie, Jaire,
Mark Wood Jr,
Aungela Wood,
Jackie Stroud-Price,
and a fan

Eddie relaxing at home

Dad & Eriq on vacation

Why would I want to go to school when I could travel across the country and around the world and see things and do things and get paid for it? So I dropped out of college to follow my musical career.

Sisters with Voices sold millions of records and made millions of dollars, but not much of it came to us. We were young, and in the middle of all that fun, no one was keeping an eye on the money. My parents were deceased, so I was out there on my own. The mother of one of the other girls passed away maybe two years into the group's success. That left us with only one parent to lend a little protection and guidance, and like any mother, she was concerned mostly with the safety and welfare of her own child. There was no one looking out for the group as a whole. The accountability was nonexistent. If I could do it all over again and know what I know now, I would be so much better off, but I was young and had nobody behind me. So when my musical career came to an end, I found myself in my midtwenties with nothing.

I met Eddie as I was on the downswing with money. I watched the bank account shrink until basically I had nothing left. I thought, I refuse to lose my condo, and so, amid stares and requests for autographs, I started looking for work. I might have been a "celebrity," but that wasn't paying any bills.

With just a high school diploma, I had limited choices, and what I found was a job as a receptionist at a coffee company that paid nine dollars an hour. Believe it or not,

I was OK with that because at least I was doing something about my situation when nobody else was. It actually gave me confidence, knowing that I was doing the right thing. I kept thinking, I haven't done anything wrong. I'm not in trouble with the law. This is just a path of life I have to walk down.

Let's just say that at that point Eddie and I had an imbalance in our finances. Here he was making millions, and I was making nine dollars an hour. But I think it kind of made him look at me differently because he would have expected some other girls just to sit there and then come to him and ask him for something. I went and got a job, and anything he did for me was because he wanted to, not because I asked him to. I guess I appeared different to him than other girls at that time.

After a few months with the coffee company, I knew I had to do something different. The bills were piling up a lot faster than the money. I made a decision to pack up everything and move to LA to try to make some real money. I wanted to take a crack at a solo singing career or an acting career. I put the condo up for sale and headed west to create a new me and start over.

Eddie was supportive. He said, "Go ahead and see what you can do. We've always been long distance, so being in LA just means a different time zone."

I tried to get on my feet, and I did everything in my power to make it work. While I was in LA, Eddie and I decided we were going to see each other more. I would scrape up money to go see him because I was afraid to ask him or tell him that I really couldn't afford that right then. It would have killed me to ask him to fly me in, so I would just say, "I can't make it." After a while he said, "You can never come here. How are we going to see each other?" And I was like, "Well, look, this is the bottom line. You know I'm trying to rebuild and I'm trying to save my money. I really can't afford a six-hundred- or seven-hundred-dollar ticket all the time." That's when he said, "I would never want you to break your bank trying to come see me. I want to see you, so I'm offering a ticket for you." What a load off of me. I didn't have to stress over flight money anymore. I knew we weren't evenly yoked at that time and I didn't want to become a burden, but he made it very clear to me that I wasn't. Whatever he did for me and whatever he gave me was because he wanted to and not because he had to. —Taj

Any time two people come into a relationship and they're both financially sound, it's a major plus, but what's even bigger is the ambition. I knew Taj was a megastar coming in, and that was attractive. I knew she was able to make a living for herself; I wasn't going to be in a situation where a woman would take advantage of me, not bringing anything to the table.

Although she fell on hard times, the ambition, the desire to succeed and grow as a human being and be the best she could be was there, and that's what I needed to see. I saw how working at some of those low-paying jobs bothered her. It hurt her to the core. People would recognize her and say, "You're working as a temp, doing this?" In Los Angeles, she didn't have a bed to sleep on. She couldn't afford it. All she had was an air mattress. That didn't bother me because of who she was and what she was striving for. I had money so we just made it happen. It never became an issue with me. I knew we'd get by. —Eddie

I worked as hard as I could in LA, but it just didn't happen. LA is kind of the end of the rainbow, and if you can't find your pot of gold there, where do you find it? In the midst of a lot of disappointment, something clicked. Why don't you go back to school, at least until your career breaks? And if by chance the career doesn't break, you'll have a new foundation of education, a way to earn enough to live on and find a little peace of mind. An education is something nobody could take away from me or squander the way the money from my singing career had been squandered. If I had an education, it would be up to me how much I accomplished.

So finally, at twenty-nine, I decided to go back to school after I'd exhausted all my efforts trying to resume my career. There's a big difference between eighteen and twenty-nine. I actually went to class every day, and I focused hard on my class work. I earned a 3.5 GPA! I completed my degree in marketing in 2004. —Taj

FINANCE AS A COUPLE

Any couple sharing a household needs to be comfortable in knowing that no matter who contributes the majority of the bread, it's still going into the same household budget. That's why we have three separate accounts—his, hers, and ours. The "ours" account is the joint account. It's the pool that needs to cover everything within the household: the mortgage, utilities, groceries, and all the basic bills, but also all the things the family does together for recreation, including vacations. And then each of us has a personal account that we can use on whatever we want. It's for life's little indulgences.

In the beginning, it's important for the two of you to establish rules on both kinds of accounts. What are we going to do with our money? How are we going to spend it? What limits are there on our own accounts?

Chances are, one partner is going to make more than the other. Still, those bills have to be covered, and there are many other ways to contribute. Among our friends is a married couple that splits the bills. An arrangement like that might well cause a problem down the road. Does it mean if one of you is short that month, you can't use the phone or the heat? It can also be problematic if a couple's spending habits are very different. Oftentimes that can lead to cracks in the relationship's foundation that make a couple feel as if they cannot combine everything in their lives. When you're married, you're a union—two becoming one. Those bills are no longer something to be split down the middle. They're something to be shared, the way everything in a marriage is shared—the good, the bad, and even the ugly!

CHANGING ROLES

There are more and more homes in which the woman is the primary earner. According to an analysis of 2005 census data performed by Andrew Beveridge, a professor of sociology at Queens College, women in their twenties earned more than their male counterparts in some large urban centers, including Dallas (120 percent), New York (117 percent), Chicago, Boston, and Minneapolis (www.reuters.com/article/2007/08/03/us-workplace-women-idUSN0334472920070803). Some men are unable to handle a situation in which their mates earn more than they do.

It's something that needs to be dealt with right up front. In those relationships, the man needs to understand that having her earning more does not emasculate him. Again, a marriage is a *we* proposition. It's *us* taking care of the family. It doesn't always have to be *me*. Situations change. Jobs and careers change. Especially in an economy like this one, there's little or nothing we can take for granted. If money has its proper place, in the context of a marriage where faith is the primary foundation, it's easier for two people to see the economic ups and downs as just part of the partnership. There are so many other ways to contribute to the household and its upkeep. Contributions of time are as important as those of money, and there's more to running a household than paying bills. There are chores to do, planning to undertake, transportation to arrange, shopping to be done, and much more.

Our financial life starts with the fact that we have to have the bills paid. Then she has her own money to spend and I have mine, and we try to come to one accord with all of that. It's set up to be clear and transparent and to help us try to avoid conflicts.

We have our talks in terms of how we're going to budget, what we need to spend and what we're going to save. There are times when we have to cut back and

times when we can treat ourselves. I like fine things, going to great restaurants, staying at the best hotels, buying good clothes, and I have to watch it from that perspective. She's always looking for a bargain, and if she wants a Louis Vuitton bag and it doesn't make sense to get it right now, she's on board with that. She won't have to have it. We were looking at getting a car recently, and basically, I said, "The timing isn't right for us to get a car right now. We have too much overhead." And there was no problem.

Through it all, we try to give ourselves freedom where we can, but we think in terms of our overall plans and what we're trying to do. —Eddie

Eddie and I have personal accounts. I happen to like Louis Vuitton bags. He loves shoes and clothes. These aren't purchases we should be making from our home account. That's our economic foundation, and we don't want to weaken that. We have "allowances," money we can spend for these indulgences. We discussed from the beginning what the reasonable limits were so that we don't have to worry about somebody doing something crazy with our family's savings.

At this point, he still makes more than I do, but we are balanced in that fact, and I add to the household as much as he does. When Eddie's NFL career ended, among some of the things he had to deal with was its effect on his feeling of self-worth. I reminded him that we're in this together! We've always been in this together, and I would never look at him as if he were any less of a man when his career or salary level changed. I would never look down on him when his situation changed, because he didn't look down on me when mine changed. I appreciated that, and I have to give him as much respect as he gave me when I was in transition. And that means if he likes that golf course and he needs to go out there sometimes and think, I say, "You go right ahead." We both came in as individuals, and keeping our fun personal accounts gives us a sense of life being a glass that is half full instead of half empty. I had to grow my finances, and he was already there, but I didn't have to get mine in order because he made me. I wanted to. I never want to feel like I can't do anything on my own or that I have to follow a rule that was not meant for me. We're both very logical, so it's nothing that's going to be outrageous, but it's always good to know that what happens with this account is up to me.

That's part of the reality of our separate accounts—we have to let each other have that freedom. Our individual decisions are just that—individual. If Eddie decides he wants something, and he's really into it, I won't complain about it. He likes to pick on me because I order workout stuff I don't always use, but I know he's being good-natured about his kidding and he doesn't tell me not to do it.

When it's something major that draws on our joint

account, then we sit down face-to-face and talk it through. When we went looking for our house, there were things each of us wanted and argued for, but they were things that fit inside the price range we had agreed on. We didn't always agree on the style of the house or the size of the yard, but after we'd looked at enough places, we found something that made us both happy.

Now, it took us three years to decorate it because we couldn't agree on things, but that's another story. Usually when that happens and we keep putting off a decision because we're not agreeing, after he's had the chance to carry on long enough, I just go ahead and make a decision, and more often than not, he'll see the new rug or drapes or countertops and say, "Oh, that is nice." —Taj

MAKING A JOYFUL LIVING

Now that we've talked about handling the money we make, it's time to talk about handling the way we make the money. What we do for a living is of profound importance. For starters, it is the way we will spend most of our waking hours during the most productive years of our lives. But it also plays into our social standing, and it is often the source of many of our friendships.

Most of us would like to make money doing something we love. The surest way for us to lead what Thoreau called "lives of quiet desperation" is to get trapped in a career we don't enjoy. "Do what you love and you'll never work a day in your life" is a common enough saying, but few people reach that seemingly magical place.

Still, it's important for us to seek employment that fulfills us. We were not put here to be miserable drudges. God intends us to enjoy our lives, and as marriage partners, we should support each other in the quest to do just that.

Both of us have had periods when we did things we loved that we were very good at and that paid us well. If that was the only time we could say that, we would still be ahead of the game. Few people get to enjoy high-profile and successful public lives.

But neither one of us would be content to rest on those laurels. We are dreamers and doers, competitive people who want to succeed and enjoy ourselves while we do.

We think it's really important for everyone to try to get to that place. We can't all be professional athletes or entertainers. We can try to seek careers or second jobs or hobbies that reflect our personalities, our dreams and desires, and as spouses, we should always be ready to offer support when our partners move in that direction. Of course, there's a realistic way to do that. We can't give up good jobs for unrealistic dreams, and our need for security grows as we get older and our families and responsibilities get larger. But there are ways to help each other feed those dreams and live more fully.

I think it's so important to search your life and find out what you love, and then learn the craft and pursue it. Taj has done that, and I really commend her for it. She wrote her own book a few years ago. She's done TV shows and has been working to develop other ones. She's still singing with her group. I try to encourage her in all of that. I don't think about it in terms of making money. I want her to be happy, and I think career is an important part of that for both of us.

It's also the approach I've taken. Since I stopped playing the game of football, I've been working hard to find the career niches that mean something to me. I've attacked that part of my life as if it's fourth and one and I see a hole developing right in front of me. I'm going all in.

The question had become, *What am I passionate about?* not *What's going to make me money?* By approaching it this way, I knew my passion would lead to financial gain. What is it that resonates with me? What is my life's purpose?

Then I asked myself the question, *What do I have?*

I said, "OK, I have a landscape architecture firm. How can I grow that business? How can I be the best at that? How can I be a better entrepreneur?"

I decided to get my MBA. I knew that stepping out of my comfort zone and putting myself in an environment where I was challenged intellectually could only work to my benefit. I took the GMAT, applied to Kellogg School of Management at Northwestern University, got tutoring sessions, and earned an MBA in the Executive MBA Program.

Life's too short to play small, so I thought, *What else do I enjoy?* I enjoy the arts. I enjoy being an entertainer whether its writing, acting, or commentating. I got with an acting coach early on and went through everything—Shakespeare, voice lessons, tap lessons—all to become an artist. If I'm going to do this, I'm going to put my all, my entire being, into it. I'm going to know and understand the craft. I'm going to embrace it and live it. I'm going to put myself into those opportunities. That's what I've been focusing on. The radio and television I'm doing relating to football keep me out there in the public eye and keep me fresh as I move further into the business and entertainment worlds.

So it's two-pronged. I'm building myself as an entrepreneur through business ventures and developing myself as an actor on stage, in TV, and in film. I'm growing in those capacities and seeing the synergies between the two.

Actually, this is something Taj and I have had to work on because we don't always see it from the same perspective. She has told me, "You don't need acting classes. Those are extracurricular." I say, "No, this is what I do now. If I want to be good at it, I've got to work that muscle."

It's like going to the gym for me. I've got to be proactive. I've got to work it so that when I do have the opportunity to shine, I'm ready. In my football days, if I had been sitting on my behind when some-body said, "We need a running back," I wouldn't have been ready. It's the same with the acting I'm pursu-ing, my business career, or anything else. You need the foundation in anything you do, and these are the things I'm pursuing in the wake of my football career. So business school was important. Acting classes are important. Not because they sound cool, not because they pass time, but because they're part of what I want to become. There are no shortcuts. It's a matter of doing the right things, putting in the time, learning the craft in all its components. And through it all, I feel like I'm being true to my passions. And that's one basis of a good, healthy, happy life—doing the things you love for a living. —Eddie

THE WORK/RELATIONSHIP BALANCE

For those of us who have both a marriage and a career, it's important that the two go hand in hand. We're not fully functioning, fully integrated people if they don't. We're the solo equivalent of a house divided against itself. And if you're successful at one but not the other, what have you really accomplished?

We have always worked to bring the two into balance. We want a happy, healthy marriage and family as well as happy, healthy careers. Getting married is about sharing your lives, and it's one of God's great gifts to us. People who aren't married can be very happy, fulfilled, and productive, but there is nothing like the opportunity to share your life experiences, the highs and lows of your quest to follow your dreams and aspirations, with a partner. Having that shared joy and that support system is a wonderful thing.

The trick is that problems in one invariably slop over onto the other. If you've got an unhappy home, you can't be as productive as a businessman or businesswoman. It's hard to maximize opportunities and reach your full potential in business if your home base isn't solid. It works the other way too. Having a chaotic business life is sure to affect your relationship because it drains your energy, steals your time, and makes it more difficult to relax and enjoy your family.

It's a delicate balancing act. Both family and business take time and attention, a sense of perspective, our best efforts, and a reliance on faith.

Balancing marriage and career is like being on a narrow beam. You don't just stand there. You're looking for balance, always adjusting, always moving. You may lean a little to the right or left, but you're always fighting for center. As you do, you begin to find and develop a rhythm that you feel comfortable with. You become one with that rhythm, that groove, and you find yourself naturally coming back to center and finding the peace within that goes with it. As you learn to breathe right, to trust your spiritual moorings, you're more likely to be of one accord with your partner and with your business. You and your partner reach that understanding when it comes to your goal and what needs to be done, so when you're applying extra time and effort to career, when you have to travel, and so on, there's no pushback. There's an understanding of what is the goal and purpose.
—Eddie

VISION

Just as a building begins with an idea in the mind of an architect, a career path or a career change begins with a vision. We've seen many people's lives upended by a lack of vision. So many athletes reaching retirement age and so many entertainers whose records aren't selling anymore are faced with the need to transition to new careers, new lives. Many of them get lost in the process. They may have been hugely successful and made millions of dollars, but without a true purpose, a vision of what life could be, they face dead ends rather than new opportunities.

Each of us has to be able to answer the question, *What am I here to do?* It's perhaps the most important question we will face. We went back to school to improve ourselves, to learn new skills. Not everyone is in a position to do that, but all of us are in a position to analyze our gifts and look for the best ways to use them.

Learning how to switch gears from pro football to the rest of my life was a difficult process for me. There were days when I wished I was still playing because it brought stability. It brought me joy. But I *wasn't* playing. That part of my life was over. So I asked, "What do I have next?" I'm constantly looking around, saying, "What's working for me? What makes me happy? What gets me

going, keeps me up at night because I'm so excited about new ideas that I can barely sleep?" With a lot of time, patience, and searching, I was able to begin the process of building the next phase of my life and career.

To be honest, I had to deprogram myself as an athlete in terms of my behaviors, but at the same time I had to rely on the principles I'd learned. I looked at the blueprint of what made me successful as an athlete. The edge is knowing the process; I understand what it takes to go through winter and summer conditioning. You don't just go into a university and say, "I'm a future Heisman Trophy winner." There's a process you have to go through, and when I arrived at Ohio State, I was in the beginning stages of that process. Now I'm in the beginning stages of my second career. I know what my goals are and what I want to accomplish, and I know I can get there, but I know it's going to take vision, patience, faith, guidance, prayer, and support. Like anyone with a long-term goal, I've got to keep that wheel turning. I've got to ignore the doubters and naysayers because they don't understand what's inside me. They haven't been there. I have to follow what's in my heart. I have to trust the process that made me a successful football player and apply its principles to what I'm doing as a businessman and an actor and all the rest. —Eddie

LET GOD DO WHAT GOD DOES

When you've done all you can do, when you've exhausted every last option, it's time to be still and let God handle the outcome. Whether it's rehearsing for a concert or negotiating a business deal, we have learned to do what we can to prepare and then let it go. God's in control anyway. We may as well let him be.

I get discouraged. I get depressed. There have been opportunities that looked promising, that I thought were going to work out but never materialized. It's hard when I experience setbacks. Sometimes I want to give up. But I've learned that when I start to have negative thoughts and face roadblocks, I need to get quiet. I rely on meditation to bring me to a calm state. And when I do, I find it hilarious that so many of us spend so much time worrying. I realize that so much of what causes worry or stress is just an illusion. I get so wrapped up in the details of things that I think I'm going to lose my mind, but when I take a good look at what they amount to, they just dissolve. I have to back away and go back to where my passion lies. I have to return to the things I can control, to the craft, and not get wrapped up in the details. That's where I find my sanity and my center again.

At other times, I'll do something I enjoy, and in those moments of relaxation and centering, the answers begin to come. *Wow,* I'll think. *I didn't look at it from this perspective. Maybe I can take care of it this way.* If I stop and listen, it rises within me organically. I feel great when that happens, realizing I don't have to depend on anybody but God for my success.
—Eddie

THE CREATIVE POWER OF WRITING

We talked in an earlier chapter about the importance of writing things down when it comes to looking at ourselves. We talked about the usefulness of a journal. But it's important to realize that kind of writing doesn't have to be limited to the problems we face or the challenges we want to overcome.

You can write down anything. It's not just about the relationships or the disappointments you have. It can be about your dreams and aspirations, capturing that creative spark inside you on paper. Writing is an opportunity to unleash your feelings and to find healing. Once you make writing a habit, you'll also be surprised at how rich a supply of ideas, thoughts, emotions, and stories will spring up inside you. One of those might well be the spark for a book or a poem or a business idea. You might be surprised at how often you say, "I could create something out of this!"

I spend a lot of time writing down the ideas I have. I have a big stack of journals. Right now I'm focused on acting, working on a one-man show based on a dream. I write down all the ideas that come up as I work through ideas in my head. It's pretty powerful stuff based on my past and the healing I've done and things like that. It's therapeutic for me, but it's an opportunity to present that and to stretch myself as an actor and a writer. It's one thing building off the other. I really encourage anyone to do that. —Eddie

MONEY AND YOU: TOOLS AND EXERCISES

It might be useful to take a moment before having a conversation about money—or about anything, really—to say a little prayer and ask God for guidance, for wisdom, and perhaps most of all, for patience, love, and understanding as you talk. Money is one of those areas where frustration, fear, and different ideas about which direction to take could make for tension or argument. Always look for a spirit of cooperation and agreement.

And don't forget that financial advisors are out there. If you can't afford an accountant or advisor, you might check with your local bank branch. After all, they're in the business of handling money and helping people save, invest, and protect theirs. Chances are, someone there would gladly sit down and offer thoughts and suggestions.

❦ What was your parents' attitude toward money? What did you learn watching them handle their finances?

❦ Does your work fulfill you? If not, do you have a long-term plan for finding a way to make a living at something that does fulfill you?

❦ Are you able to live within your means?

❦ Are you willing to write up a budget and stick to it?

❧ Have you read books or articles or online pieces about handling money?

❧ Do the two of you talk about your finances? Can you remain calm and constructive as you do so?

❧ Do you have a short-term game plan when it comes to money?

❧ Do you have long-term goals? Do you agree on them?

❧ Have you thought about and begun planning for your retirement?

❧ Are you able to set a little aside from each paycheck to save or invest?

🦋 Do you have one joint account for household bills?

🦋 Can you view money as something with a spiritual component?

🦋 Can you control impulse buys?

🦋 When you do have financial problems, are you able to solve them together by talking, planning, and acting?

🦋 If not, would you consider getting professional help or advice?

One way to foster discussion about finances is to share what you're reading. Clip or mark the interesting or useful articles you run across or print out pieces you find online and share them with each other. It's a good way to see where your ideas line up and where they differ. It's also a great way to find out what the experts are thinking. You might share money-saving tips as well—coupons from the Sunday paper, more comparison shopping, and putting off any purchase that isn't essential. And in times like these, it's not a bad idea to include a request for peace of mind even in the midst of economic uncertainty as you pray, alone or together.

CHAPTER FIVE

PRACTICE THE ART OF SEX

The true art of sex is learning real intimacy. What we think of when we say "sex" is just one part of the equation. Strangers have sex. People in healthy relationships, in good marriages, can achieve true intimacy, and sex is a beautiful and loving celebration of that achievement. When two people experience intimacy on every level—emotional, mental, spiritual—then the physical act ties it all together, and sex becomes the incredible gift that God gave Adam and Eve and all the rest of us. It is the pinnacle of the expression of a couple's oneness.

In the early days of a marriage, it's no surprise that sex is probably a bigger part of a couple's communication than it may ever be again. As time goes by and couples get a little older, as the demands of making a living and keeping a household get bigger, as the family starts to expand, sex can get pushed into the corner. Sometimes in the midst of all those responsibilities it seems there are barely enough hours in the day to brush your teeth before bed, let alone enough for a great sex life.

Sex is incredibly important, though, and there's an art to

keeping it fresh. It doesn't take hours and hours or long, steamy nights. We're not discounting those things, but most of us have to work for a living and raise kids. We have to find a way to make sex a part of what already seems like a full plate.

We want to look at some little techniques—not sex techniques, but methods and suggestions—for keeping that spark alive. This chapter will help longtime couples rediscover the simple moments that keep those fires burning and help new couples look for the kind of perspective that will enable them to establish a love life that will last.

Placing an overemphasis on the physical side of a relationship early could potentially invite trouble. Sex is a pleasurable activity, but if you're not careful with it, it can hurt you. It can be distracting. It can cloud your judgment. It can be addictive. And when it's not treated as the serious element of a relationship that it is, it can lead to all kinds of misconstrued emotions and complications. That's why we've stressed the importance of self-discovery and communication. You need to be knowledgeable about yourself and about your partner before sex becomes part of the equation. There must be a mutual understanding of what it means to be committed to each other, and the Bible is right in saying that an intimate relationship is best expressed within marriage. We know that now, but we are also older and wiser now. Sex is in a very real sense a point of no return. There's no regaining that pre-sexual status. The element of surprise is gone. Your innocence has been taken. If you're not ready for it, you're in new territory without a useful map.

The two of us were in different cities for much of the early part of our relationship. For those of you in close proximity, who see a lot of each other, it's worth taking it slow. The physical element of your relationship should not be your primary concern. It should be placed somewhere down the line because it can easily overcome everything else.

If you have already crossed that boundary, it's still possible to start all over. We did. When we decided to become engaged, we went into premarital counseling. Our counselor told us we should practice abstinence for the nine months that remained until the wedding. We did our best to do just that. It's the hardest thing we ever did because we were so used to touching each other. Plus, we lived together, so you had two people living in the same house who were literally not having any kind of physical attachment. Sometimes just hugging each other was too much of a temptation. We'd be like, "Oh, get away from me!"

Our counselor suggested that if that task was too hard, one of us should move out. We are very cheap at times. We were like, "Now, if you move out, we're going to have to pay rent in addition to the mortgage when we have this big house! You go downstairs." The amount of travel we were doing helped, but it still took determination. You have to look at it as wiping the slate clean. You start from scratch and remove that element. If you can do that, you'll be better off.

When we got married, we went straight to making up for lost time. It may not be surprising to hear that our son Eriq was conceived on our honeymoon!

AN EXPRESSION OF HOLINESS

Too many people regard sex as being outside of or separate from the holiness of a relationship, but it's not! It's the ultimate expression of the holiness of the relationship. When you get married in a church and you swear to love and cherish each other " 'til death do us part," you've entered into a partnership ordained by God. Your love is blessed by God, and it's so important to show that love only to your partner. Since yours is a spiritual union, anything you do within that union has a spiritual component.

It's also important to recognize that sex is a very strong need. It is an inborn, physical yearning that needs expression one way or another. After all, God created Eve for Adam. That was God's plan all along. Eve was placed with Adam to provide companionship, help, conversation, and pleasure—just about everything. Our bodies are designed to complement each other as well as to procreate.

Recognizing the strength of that urge is what led Paul to say, "It is better to marry than to burn" (1 Corinthians 7:9 KJV). By "burn," he meant "burn with passion." It can be a pretty demanding urge, and we see it cause a lot of problems when misdirected to things like pornography and cheating.

We're firm believers that sex needs expression and that married couples have to work to find those moments when they can push it to the front burner. Just as couples need to find time to spend together to talk and to have fun, they need to find time for physical love, even if it's just a moment to connect physically without getting to all-out sex. You want to find little things to keep that spark going.

There are so many ways to make love, to express love physically. That's where the art comes in. It could be the touch of a hand, a kiss on the forehead, a firm caress. It could be a long, passionate kiss and a loving look in each other's eyes. It could be something she wears, a wink, a stare from across the room. It can be anything that shows your mate that you are still physically attracted to him or to her. Those are the little moments that will keep the fire burning in a relationship. We all need those times with our mates. They let us have a sense of being needed and wanted and loved, all those things you get from the intimate part of a relationship. They will make a man and a woman hurry through rush-hour traffic because there's something fun waiting at home.

Then there are the signals you can use with each other, things that become your private language of love. Say you know you're going to get home before the kids do on a certain day. You might lay a rose on the bed. You might leave a lipstick print on a note on the table. Communication is so important in expressing love, whether it's one of those moments-in-passing or a lengthy session when you've finally found some time and space. You need to know your mate well enough to know how best to express your love physically. You also need to be able to communicate the things you like, not to remain silent or hold back, but to be open and free.

What you're striving for is that place where it's easy to express your needs and to know and meet your partner's. Everything you have, all of the elements in your relationship, can come together in a fun and satisfying way when you connect with your mate physically. But it takes an ongoing commitment to that place where a touch and a glance and a spoken word can all be part of your physical expression of love.

I consider anything we do in terms of expressing our love to be an outpouring of thankfulness to God for bringing us together. So I make sure—and at times I may drive him crazy—that now and then I come up behind Eddie and I just hug him, or I walk up to him and say, "Hold me!" And we just hold each other. He'll say, "Are you OK today?" and I'll tell him, "I'm great," or "I'm glad you're home." With his touch, I feel the presence of something wonderful and profound because it's a love that can't be broken.

Those moments may seem like such little things, but given the realities of people's schedules, it's hard to spend hours and hours together. I think a lot of people could avoid couples therapy if they'd just recognize the importance of those little moments. They count!

And it's so important to try to enjoy sex with your mate and not feel like you have to do it because he or she wants you to do it. It shouldn't feel like an obligation. It should be something that you enjoy and want to do.

Eddie and I have mastered the art of loving on each other on the go! I mean, I'm on the road half the time, and during the season he's gone. Sometimes we only see each other once a week. You have to find a moment to say "I love you" physically without going into a routine. You have to keep it fresh, and that's what we try to do. Eddie will walk up to me and grab me a certain way, and I know what's going to happen.

A woman who's working, going to school, taking care of the kids, whatever her obligations are, can't be super-woman all the time, but she can be speed girl, you know? I mean, there has to be a way to balance it without wearing her out while keeping him satisfied, so the two of you can know that you still love each other, that you still have this great physical connection. —Taj

Sex is about chemistry, and my wife and I are to the point where I don't have to say a word. She knows how to touch me, what I like. The disconnect comes in when you lose connectivity or the passion or the communication. That's where you get out of sync.

Knowing where your partner is sexually is so important. You have to read your partner, understand his or her moods. Sex is about timing, knowing what to do, how to do it, and when to apply it. If you can stay open and honest in terms of your sex life, in communicating what turns you on, trust me, it makes a world of difference. And if you can't be who you are, in sex as in anything else, basically you can't be in a relationship.

The thing I struggle with sometimes is stopping to express day-to-day love and affection. It's something I continue to work on. I try to be conscious of how important it is to stop and give her a kiss or do something else that says, "I'm thinking about you." There are times when I'm in a rush or really tired, when I may be distracted and not want to play or be touched. I have a tendency to be a little too hard. But she can take me in another direction to where I'll give her a hug, hold her, rub her back, make her feel special, let her know "You're my baby. I love you." I'm trying to become better at that. —Eddie

Our pasts have such a profound influence on us. We've spent a great deal of time talking about that fact and suggesting questions and exercises that can help you face, deal with, and use your past to the best advantage. And it's important to acknowledge that the things in our backgrounds that affect us spiritually or emotionally can easily affect us sexually. Often it's in terms of self-esteem. People bring different kinds of dysfunction to a marriage. They can hold back from each other because of fear left over from childhood trauma. They can use sex to run from other forms of intimacy.

Having a healthy adulthood includes working on ourselves so that our approach to sex is as healthy as our approach to faith or money.

I see pieces of her past affect Taj to this day. She recently said to me, "I just now looked at pictures from when I was younger, and I just realized I was beautiful." Think about her self-esteem when it came to dealing with me at the time! I was looking at her as, *You are gorgeous.* **She didn't see that. She was sending back a negative image that grew out of how she saw herself. She was not giving her beautiful self to me. In her mind, subconsciously, it was this protected, ugly person she thought she was. It was all**

there in how she viewed herself, which was an out-growth of the self-perception she learned or didn't learn as a young girl.

I brought in baggage of my own. In the beginning, I wanted Taj, but I still wanted to meet and talk to other women and experience other relationships. It's just where I was at that time. I didn't want to lose the gem I had in Taj, but part of me still wanted to be a playboy. I held her at arm's length to some degree.

My perception of a relationship wasn't a healthy one. There were ways in which my own self-esteem and my relationship issues blocked us from having a deeper love. I wanted to have my cake and eat it too. I enjoyed my life as a single man. Part of me didn't want to let that go, but something deep inside of me said it's not sustainable, that life has no gravitas. I had let go of the hurt and pain that I experienced in life. I realized that what I was doing wasn't healthy and was not leaving a strong legacy. That experience gave me the opportunity to appreciate my wife and love her fully.

Being attracted to other women is something I don't think you ever conquer. I understand and accept that. However, I understand that, for me, it's a defense mechanism that grew out of the baggage I brought into the relationship. It wasn't anything mali-cious. It came from my own experiences. I have to deal with that the rest of my life, although I approach and perceive it differently now. I've come to understand that I can't control the thoughts that come into my head, but I can control what stays. And I have to make the right choice.

Becoming faithful is a process; it's like working out. The more you work on it, the stronger it becomes. Through prayer, Scripture, and conscious living, you give yourself a chance. The only thing I can guarantee is giving my best and respecting my marriage on a daily basis. The most important thing to me now is my family. I do know Taj has got my back. She's in the foxhole with me, through and through. It has taken me time to realize, "You've got a special woman in your life. Don't take that for granted." I did take that for granted in the past, but now I understand the special woman I have in my life. She has been there beside me as I've entered this new phase. That means everything to me. —Eddie

There's one more thing it's really important to mention about sex, and it's an extension of something we talked about earlier. As we've said, sex at its best is an expression of a spiritual union, but it definitely involves our bodies. Both of us know that being fit physically keeps the attraction level and the sex drive up. It keeps you excited and turned on.

The same things that we spoke about then apply here. We need to take care of our bodies. That involves nutrition, exercise, and relaxation, among other things. Taking care of these is a sure way to improve your health, your self-image, and your sex life.

YOUR SEX LIFE: TOOLS AND EXERCISES

Gaining a balanced and healthy view of sex will go a long way toward improving any relationship. It's part of the building block of attraction, and it was built into the way men and women see each other. But it can't overwhelm a relationship. That's why we talked in an earlier chapter about getting to know each other as complete human beings and realizing that sex isn't the way to do that. At the same time, sex, both in the act itself and in the day-to-day intimacy it fosters and represents, is a vital component of a healthy marriage.

Nothing can kill physical intimacy like a lack of communication. Sex is an extension of communication, and it's worth talking about. Making love starts way before you get to the bedroom. Your exercises here involve making sure you're on the same page—even when, as a man and a woman, your physiological and mental approaches to sex might be a little different. Here are some questions worth thinking through and, most important, talking about.

❧ Did you grow up with a healthy perception of sex?

🦋 Are there things in your background that affect the way you view sex?

🦋 Has either of you faced abuse or other traumas that still affect you?

🦋 Do you think you have sex in its proper perspective within your relationship?

🦋 Do you and your partner express affection easily?

🦋 Do you show affection unconnected with sex?

🦋 Do you find ways to make your partner feel special?

🦋 Can you talk freely about sex with your partner?

🦋 Are you able to express your wishes and desires when it comes to sex?

🦋 Are you able to view sex as part of the spiritual side of your relationship, as a sacred expression of your bond?

🦋 Are you sometimes so busy or distracted that you push a healthy sex life to the side?

🦋 Do you find yourselves arguing about how often you make love?

🦋 Does sex still feel special to both of you?

🦋 Can you trust each other in sexual matters when you're apart?

🦋 Might you benefit from counseling about sex?

CHAPTER SIX

BUILD THE POWER OF ONE

We have been talking throughout this book about the practical and straightforward process by which any couple can build a loving, powerful life together. We hope that you've seen what real people with less-than-ideal backgrounds and work-in-progress personalities—that would be all of us!—can accomplish with some work and a few simple tools.

So, if you're willing to put in the time and effort, what can you expect? In this chapter we'll talk about the destination, that place where two people come together and truly express themselves as one. We'll deal with what happens when a couple forms a real union, the kind that is the basis of a fully functioning family.

As we've seen, it's not about becoming perfect. Lord knows the two of us aren't, and we don't plan on getting there soon! But if you are honestly working on the areas of your life together that we've been talking about, you can form a partnership that is bigger and better than the sum of its parts. You'll arrive at a place where you're able to work through your differences at home and present a unified front to the world, a place where you always know you've got each other's back.

We have come to call that place the Power of One. Put simply, it's a united structure, built step by step on a foundation of faith, from which you live the rest of your lives together. It's the place from which you'll draw the strength to weather life's storms as a couple.

Every building begins with a vision. So does every successful marriage partnership. And just as a building can't have two architects working separately, a successful marriage can't have two dreamers pulling in different directions. That's why we've emphasized the importance of working on yourself, to make sure you're ready to move from *I* to *we*, and why we've provided questions and discussion starters to help get both of you on the same page and keep you there on the most important topics facing couples.

Of course, partners may have separate careers or hobbies or friends, but the marriage itself, the base from which all of those things operate, must share a common vision that unites the two individuals. Once you've gotten there—and we wrote this book to tell you in no uncertain terms that you *can*—you'll experience a better relationship than you thought possible as you come to know the joy of the Power of One.

We caught our first glimpses of what life together could be like while we were dating. It happened as we honestly started working on ourselves as individuals and as a couple. Then, when the time came, all the work that we put into our relationship made our wedding an occasion of unbridled joy. It was the most incredible day of our lives.

We were married in a beautiful garden in perfect weather. I love pink, so we had pink everywhere. The music, the food, the atmosphere, everything was just the way you'd want it.

The best part of it was that when we went off on our honeymoon, I felt that I was there with the person I should have been on my honeymoon with. There was no question that I married the man created to be my husband. I was extremely grateful. And for good measure, don't forget we were coming off nine months of celibacy!

Because we had worked on ourselves, both of us were at a point where we could give ourselves completely to each other and become a couple. Two could become one. And because we continued to do the work after we married, we formed a unified front. That didn't mean we were never going to disagree, but it meant that we had a full and loving partnership, the Power of One, as our goal and that we were willing to work to accomplish and maintain that.

Eddie is my soul mate. I can't imagine being with anybody else. I feel that everything I went through prior to meeting Eddie was to prepare me for him, and when we finally met, everything just fell into place. —Taj

There are so many things that attracted me to Taj. Her work ethic was one of the first. I saw it even when she was struggling. She always had a plan, and she was always working to make it happen. She's determined that way. Then there are her values. They're strong—very strong. I could never imagine starting a family with someone who didn't have that. She makes a wonderful mother. She's an anchor. She's committed, and she believes in the things that I believe in. She's a survivor, literally and figuratively, and she has a great balance between being tough and being sweet. Those are the great qualities I see in her. And all of that emanates through her smile, her eyes, and her overall look. Her inner being just enhances the physical beauty she has already. —Eddie

The process of building and maintaining a family unit never happens in a vacuum. There are other family members, social pressures, job stresses, and all the other things that make up real life. That's why it's so important for a couple to have a united place to stand.

Many of us have family members who are quick to offer advice, stir up controversy, criticize, or otherwise complicate our lives. Their comments, well meaning or not, can easily lead to discord. You don't want to be drawn into conversations that reflect negatively on you, on your partner, or on you as a couple. Presenting a unified front is a surefire way to fend off those kinds of problems. Say you are the woman in a relationship and his Aunt Mary is always putting down your abilities as a cook or housekeeper. It's best just not to take the bait. If you're living the Power of One, you and your spouse have talked through your approach to housekeeping—and everything else about your relationship—and you're on the same page. And if you are, that's all you need to say. "He's happy with me, and I'm happy with him" is plenty. If Aunt Mary doesn't get the message, arguing isn't the solution. Your best course of action is to try never to give in to outside negativity. Remember, you can't control someone else's attitude, but you are in full control of yours.

Your opinions of each other are the ones that count, and good communication between you is the best defense against the gossips and bad-mouthers all of us run into at some point.

Many families these days are blended families. That means exes and children from other relationships may well play intimate roles in your lives. First and foremost, these children have to feel welcomed, loved, and nurtured. Nothing is tougher on a child than the sense that he or she is unwanted, bothersome, or less than. Couples have to take special pains to work through any problems along those lines.

Once we were married, we were a complete family. We started with a firm foundation we built together—just the two of us. Nothing was going to come between us—not family, not friends, not finances, not anything. Then, from the beginning, our family included Eddie's son Jaire, who was seven when Eddie and I were married. I have always considered him my son as well, even though I'm not his biological mom. It has never felt like he's coming to visit us when he comes for summers or holidays. It feels like he is coming home.

As for my younger son, Eriq, he has so many of Eddie's tendencies and so many of mine. He's going to be stubborn with a sensitive side. Last Father's Day I put together a video of the boys and Eddie. At first, Eriq was watching it and smiling, and then out of nowhere he was sobbing. When I asked him what was wrong, he said, "I'm happy!" I'm very glad he has Eddie's big heart—he's always giving things away. And then he has his stubborn side like his mommy. He just has to do things his way, even if he gets hurt. When he does, I'll say, "Now can we try it Mommy's way?" On the other hand, he wants to hold my hand, and he'll open doors for me. He loves to kiss as well. When he knows he's in trouble, he'll say, "Kisses?" like he's saying, "Can one of my kisses fix this?" He's going to be a great boyfriend. Every girl is going to think she's the one. Every girl.

Jaire is fourteen now and Eriq is six, and both are completely consumed with being kids because they don't have *anything else to deal with. They don't have to deal with Mommy's and Daddy's baggage, because we've packed up and gotten rid of most of it, and what's left we deal with on our own, as two adults. We really think that's the way it should be. —Taj*

If the Power of One can't help a couple through the biggest problems that can come along, there's not much point in working to achieve it. Life, as we've said, is a contact sport, and it can bang us up, as individuals and as couples. Health problems, family crises, accidents, career changes, and all sorts of other challenges are out there waiting. But we know from experience that it's possible to use the exercises and techniques we've talked about in this book to handle *whatever* happens.

Most of what couples face comes down to problems with money, sex, and family, and we've talked in detail about dealing with these. But big or small, a lot of problems can be avoided if we'll just give each other two things everybody needs in abundance—space and support. Couples can learn over time how to provide each other with both and, perhaps more important, when to provide which!

The two of us have separate ways of dealing with the stress that pops up in our lives, as it does in every life and in all relationships. We've also learned how to offer comfort and stress relief to each other when it's wanted and how to back off when it isn't.

Space can be as simple as granting some time alone, but it might also mean postponing a discussion about a sensitive subject until your partner is ready. *Support* can be as simple as a kiss or a touch that says, "Yep, I still love you," or as all-consuming as the willingness to sacrifice time, money, and sleep to help your spouse get through school or start a business. Each couple has to decide what's right in those circumstances, although sometimes if problems arise because one or both of you are unclear about when or whether to provide space or support, it's worthwhile getting an outside opinion from a trusted friend, family member, or counselor.

Even married people need time apart, and Eddie and I get plenty of it because of our separate careers. When we're both at home, we have our favorite individual activities, ways we unwind, or friends we hang with now and then. We're both great about letting the other have space. Eddie might head to the basement to practice his DJ skills, playing his favorite songs, and on nice days I love to wash my truck—really! I call her Big Sylvia, and I get out my detailing kit: the hose and all my soaps, waxes, chamois, and all

the rest. I go to the Y to work out, and Eddie heads to the golf course with his buddies. We have our own ways to unwind, to stay in shape, and to make our time together that much better. —Taj

We both have our own little processes for burning off stress. And we're good at picking up each other's cues. I know that if she's mad about something, I should stay out of her way. Then at the right time, I'll try to talk about it to get to the root of the problem and try to move forward if I can. The same if she's been working really hard and is just tired. She likes to get her rest in her own way, and I just let her. I'll show her that I'm there if she needs me—I'll try to massage her or just hold her for a minute—but I pretty much know when to let her deal with it on her own.

When I need to unwind, I DJ in the house. I'll go downstairs and play music—loud—for hours. Just listening to music inspires me. That's my escape, what I love to do. If I want to work on technique or timing, I put weights on my wrist. I just play what feels right according to the mood I'm in. There are also things I enjoy that require me to get out of the house, like golf. Both are just part of who I am, and all of this is about doing things you love to do and

having the space and the outlets to do them in order to be happy and fulfilled. —Eddie

Eddie doesn't get down very often, and even when he does, he doesn't show it that much. Earlier this year, when he was up for the NFL Hall of Fame and he didn't make the first cut, it angered me to no end. Of course, I'm the one who usually blows up. He's like, "Just relax, relax. It's OK. I'll get there eventually, just not this year." I said, "I don't wanna hear that. I want you there today! I wanna go and wear a new dress and look cute when you go up there." He just cracks me up because he's always the one to talk me off the ladder. When he does get down, all he wants is to be held. He just wants to lie down. He sleeps on everything. He'll just sleep it off and come back the next day ready, and if he does get whiny like that, I'll just lie down with him and encourage him and tell him that it will pass. I tell him he's the greatest and nothing could ever touch him 'cause he's my babe. By the next day, we're back to normal. —Taj

Support can take all kinds of forms, but the bottom line for us is mutual respect. We encourage each other to stretch, to reach, to dream. We've watched each other scale the heights of our professions since our first days together, and we still have as much confidence and belief in each other as we do in ourselves, no matter what we're undertaking. We also know very well that success for one is success for both. We're encouraged by each other's progress, and we're uplifted by each other's accomplishments. That's part of the Power of One—the success of either makes both of us better, happier, and more fulfilled.

A few years ago Eddie decided he wanted to go to graduate school. I said, "Sure," not realizing how intense it was going to be. He was gone every other week, and he was also working. We hardly saw each other for two years! It was a tough struggle, but watching him do that inspired me to start following my dream about law school. I was like, "Why can't I? If he can go back to school to get his management degree, I can do it with a law degree." And he's like, "Go for it. We'll manage. We'll find a way to keep the kids engaged." We basically support each other. And he told me, "If you find you don't like it once you get there, you don't have to go anymore. It's OK."

He's always been supportive and level-headed like that

when I've asked for advice. There have been times when my career wasn't going smoothly, and I'd complain and complain to him, and one time he said, "Do it because you want to, not because you have to, because you don't." And that was the best thing he ever said to me about my career. It made it so much easier for me. It was really liberating. —Taj

THE AMERICAN DREAM

A lot of people think we're living the American dream, and to some extent we are, but living the American dream does not guarantee happiness twenty-four hours a day. For some reason, people think we don't have arguments or get annoyed with each other or have any of the other troubles that couples have. We do. But we make it a point to express ourselves, to work through those things in private, within the safe walls of our house. That way, when we step outside, we've left the disagreements behind, and we present a united front. The Power of One doesn't mean the rough edges are smoothed off and nothing ruffles either of you. It means you work through those things and then go out and live life as a team.

After we had done our TV show (I Married a Baller on TV One), so many people would e-mail and tell us how great they thought we were. People tell me that in airports everywhere I go, and it cracks me up because I'm thinking, They just need to live with him! I love him to death, but he's not perfect! He's messy and he loves to overcommit and it drives me crazy. He says yes to everyone. Not long ago I had to go in for my third knee surgery in three years, and he was going to drive me there. But sometime between talking to me about it and the actual day, someone asked him to do something at the same time my surgery was scheduled and he said yes. That's just Eddie. Ironically, that's one of the things I love about him. His heart is so big, he doesn't know how to say no. We did work that one out and he did take me, but I'm like, "Just try saying no once. It works. It really does." But he still doesn't do it. So he's not perfect, but then again I feel as though there's nothing that I can't tolerate. Even when I want to kill him, I can tolerate him! —Taj

We talk a lot about the *work* that goes into a successful relationship; but once you're under way, it's every bit as important to make sure you *enjoy* the little corner of the American dream you're able to carve out for yourselves. Treasure the laughter, the conversations, the meals together, the date nights, the kids, the soccer games, the vacations—all of it. And remember to thank God for it. As believers, we know we are relying on God's power to get all of this accomplished. It's his blessings we are celebrating here. Marriage is one of God's greatest gifts to us. It comes with responsibilities and it's filled with challenges, but it is meant to be a source of joy and strength.

You definitely have to be persistent about pursuing the American dream because it very seldom just falls at your feet or lands on your doorstep. Even the people you think this happened to have gone through a lot more than you suspect. In the case of my career, sometimes I look at my surroundings, the things I have now, and I think about how long it took me just to believe it! I never thought anything like this would happen. No matter how hard I tried, I guess I just didn't dream big enough. I was happy with just one song on the radio. But to have almost a dozen singles and sell seven million records and have people almost twenty years later still singing those songs—even in countries where they can't say hi in English but they can sing every word!—it's mind-blowing at times. And I might have been happy with a relationship that was somewhat functional, but look who—and what—I wound up with! I'm grateful

every day about that part of my life. So the American dream is definitely attainable if you're persistent, and depending on how big you dream, you just never know what can happen.

The future is wide open. I still love performing, interacting with the crowd, especially when they're really hyped. That just makes me grow wings, and I'm all over the place. I ALWAYS want to be in the music industry. I have a marketing degree, and once I get my law degree I'm hoping to do sports and entertainment law. I want to combine those two and continue the dream in that way.

Of course, I have to say that there's no magic wand. All of this is happening in the real world. I knew I was going to be taking the LSAT, the Law School Admission Test, but I have a schedule that isn't very conducive to studying. I was in Japan for eight days, and then I was scheduled to start taking the Kaplan test preparation course upon my return. I took a twenty-two-hour flight home from Japan and arrived in Nashville at three in the afternoon. My son wanted to watch a movie with me. I couldn't say no—my child had not seen me in over a week! I was sitting there half asleep with him. Then I had to go to class from six to ten. The classes met on Sunday, Tuesday, and Thursday from two to six and six to ten, and in between that I was still traveling and performing, my son had developed walking pneumonia, my sister was having health problems that prevented her from driving, and Eddie had just had knee surgery. I was the only mobile person in the house, so I was *taking my sister for EEGs and taking Eddie to his follow-up appointments and rehab and also taking care of my son, thinking, If I do well on this test, I'm really smart.*

After an intense month of study, I was finally prepared to take the test, which is a long, long six-parter, and it pretty much reinforced any leftover low self-esteem I had. I was thinking, Why in the world am I doing this to myself? I left there drained, but I can say that in spite of everything at least I did it! —Taj

THE MAN AND THE WOMAN OF THE HOUSE

When we're at home, we leave all the expectations other people have of us outside. Once we are within that sacred and protected space, we get to determine what our relationship is and what its ground rules are. It's important for every couple to find the place where both parties are comfortable that way. We try to make the rules—even those we lay out in this book—fit us. We try to be patient and respect each other. We don't make judgments too fast, especially negative judgments. We try to stay open to possibilities. And we give each other room to grow.

We know women and men who seem to be happily married but

who say things like, "I'd like to do that, but he (or she) won't let me," or "He (or she) took that away from me." It's hard for either of us to imagine being in a relationship like that. That's one person thinking for both. That's one person losing his or her voice, and without a voice you can't be completely happy.

Marriage shouldn't be a prison. It should be liberation. Yes, marriage is something you abandon yourself to, but in doing so, you embrace a new and wonderful freedom within a world of love and growth and opportunity.

Both of us have been in the public eye since the day we met, Eddie as an athlete and me as an entertainer. We're still those people, but these days Eddie is an entrepreneur, an actor, and a commentator, and I'm a recording artist, an author, and a businesswoman, among other things. But none of those careers follows us into the house. There, it's just Eddie and Taj. Home is where I can let my hair down. I don't have to get made up if I don't want to. We can just be us, good, bad, or indifferent. Home is our sanctuary.

Within that sanctuary, my husband is "the head" of our household. That's something I don't want to be. I believe in the prescription given in Ephesians: "The husband is the head of the wife, even as Christ is the head of the church." But it doesn't end there. It goes on to say, "Husbands, love your wives, even as Christ also loved the church, and gave himself for it" (Ephesians 5:23, 25 KJV). It calls for love and sacrifice as well as headship. Too many people quote the first part and forget the rest. I want both parts in place.

And there is so much more to the husband-wife relationship. There is mutuality, first and foremost. I don't take away his manhood by aspiring to take over his position as head of the household, and at the same time he can't take away my roles as wife, mother, and career person. I came into our relationship with my career, and it is still an important part of me. In fact, when we started dating, he was a fan. It's obvious I had adjustments to make in becoming his girlfriend, and given our histories, both of us had some tweaking to do. But those adjustments did not include having me negate who I am or go into a shell because I became his girlfriend and then his wife. That's not what a relationship is about.

There are plenty of things we disagree about. We even have a little drama now and then. But those disagreements don't turn into long, drawn-out fights. He'll say, "I don't think you should do it that way," and I might say, "What are you talking about? Look at it this way." At some point, though, one of us will say, "Well, let me think about that." We're willing to consider the other opinion and the other side of the question. That's the goal—to let the feelings wear off a little and then think things through. If we have a disagreement and we can't settle it right there, we walk away, and eventually we come back with a little better perspective.

But I know a lot of people are thinking, Well, who has the final say? The answer is, "We do." I'm too independent for him to have control of me, and he's a man—I can't control him. I don't want him to feel like I'm his mother. I'm his wife. I don't demand things. I don't say, "It's my way or no way." We talk about it. If he sees that I feel strongly about something, he'll do it my way. If he's dead set on something, I'll let him have it. No one rules my house, but he is the man of the house, and I respect and love him as such.

Eddie and I recognize each other's strengths and respect each other's roles. He knows I'm the person who gets things done. I keep the house together. If he has an appointment, I get him up on time. He may be the man of the house, but he tells me all the time that I'm the general. —Taj

WORKING TOGETHER

We thought it was funny when this book came along because we hardly ever work together. That's not surprising when you get to know us, because I can't do anything athletic and he definitely can't sing! So we thought it was really cute that we could spend some time together on this book. It has been a new adventure—fun and really cool.

It started as an idea I had for a little manual that would be useful to people in the situation I'd been in—needing some guidance on making love work. Then together we set out to capture a picture of a complete and mature relationship that people can aspire to.

Part of what cracks us up is that we have such different personalities, yet we're so similar. We bring different backgrounds and perspectives to this book, but we agreed on the final product. And we're both looking forward to getting out there and speaking together, talking to people about the book and the ideas in it.

Getting the chance to help people, providing a road map to a happier, healthier marriage, is important because it wasn't always peaches and cream for us. And once again— we're not perfect now. If he gets on my nerves, I'll tell him. When we're out with friends and he annoys me, I'll pop him on the back of his head, although people think it's cute when I do that. I think that's part of our "couple" personality. We have arguments, but we work them out behind the scenes.
—Taj

WHERE WE GO FROM HERE

We're still dreaming, and the future looks bright to both of us because there's nothing that says we can't do everything we set out to do, even at this point. Eddie and I run on parallel paths, although he is more organized about it than I am. He visualizes everything by putting quotations, *ideas, and thoughts up on his vision board. He's working toward his health initiative, which I think is so great, and I'm working on my career as far as the music is concerned and my dream of being an attorney, and down the line developing that into something more.*

All of it begins with our togetherness, though. That's our platform. Everything starts here, and then he can branch off and do his things and I can branch off and do mine, but we'll always have this path that comes back together. Because of that, when I look into the future, I see us building our family and what we consider our empire to heights we've never dreamed of. —Taj

There are so many parallels between building a career and building a home and family. You need the right people involved. You need to have a solid foundation in place and a workable plan for going vertical with the things you want to accomplish. And you want to choose your measures of success carefully. Are they financial? To some degree, they may be. Do they involve being happy with what you do, with not feeling like it's work? Absolutely!

When it comes to career, I'm still in that stage of creating and refining the message, finding and massaging the foundation so I can go vertical. But all of it is built on what I've established, beginning with the dreams of my childhood years, through my life in sports and now into my career after my playing days. Everything I'm doing with George Enterprises I see through the lens of health and wellness, whether it's a fitness center or a health venture or my landscape architecture firm focusing on creating healthier places, economically, socially, and environmentally. I can see bringing these themes to light via documentaries, plays, one-man shows, and other projects, so what I do in the entertainment world, from acting to radio, helps polish that part of my skill set.

When it comes to home and family, I've had to improve on what I saw as a child. I've had to find something better to aim at and then work to accomplish that. Choosing someone who shared that vision and was willing to work on it with me made the dream achievable. Sharing the common goal helps us put everything that comes up—good and bad—in perspective.

For Taj and me, this book is a chance to strike a chord with people, and we're looking forward to traveling and to speaking engagements that will let us carry a message of hope and wellness on all fronts.

There is something wonderful in knowing that we have yet to explore all the possibilities. There is so much more to discover in terms of things we can create as a team, personally, entrepreneurially, and philanthropically. I can see the level of joy and fulfillment

we experience just getting greater all the time too. After all these years as a couple, there's so much more to tap in to. In fact, I think we're just scratching the surface. —Eddie

THE POWER OF ONE: TOOLS AND EXERCISES

The questions here *are* the exercise. This chapter is specifically about the way it all comes together as two become one. So you're going to go through these questions twice—once by yourself and once as a couple. Write down your answers so you can refer to them as you and your partner go through them again. See where you line up and where you don't, and do your best to figure out where that's okay and where you need work to line up more closely. After all, you're building and strengthening a partnership that makes you a better you as you become a more fulfilled, more aligned couple.

Who are the people among your family and friends who build you up as a couple, whose influence is pretty much always good? Do you seek them out? Do you nurture these friendships and relationships?

🦋 Who are the people whose influence is negative? Are you able to minimize their roles in your life? Are you able to react as a unified couple?

🦋 What does your mate want when he or she is disappointed or down? What do you want? Compare the two. See if you're offering what the other wants.

🦋 What do you do to unwind as a couple? What do you do individually? Is there balance there?

🦋 What are the dreams you still have to pursue as an individual? Does your partner know about them? Encourage them?

🦋 What dreams does your spouse still have to pursue? Do you encourage those you know about?

❧ How about the dreams you share? A dream house? A vacation? The occasional romantic weekend away?

❧ Do you take time to enjoy your relationship? Have you ever just spent a little time talking about the good things you have?